Making Time Work For You

Books by Harold L. Taylor

Personal Organization: The Key to Managing Your
Time and Your Life

Managing Your Memory

Delegate: The Key to Successful Management

Making Time to Sell

Manage Your Meetings

The Educated Executive

Getting Organized

28 Time Problems and How to Solve Them

The Administrator's Guide to Effective Time
Management

Time Worp: 750 Ways to Save Time

Say Yes To Your Dreams

Procrastinate Less & Enjoy Life More

2010 Time Tips

A guide to productive time management

Making Time Work For You

HAROLD L. TAYLOR

**Revised & expanded edition of the classic
time management bestseller**

First published in March, 1981 by
General Publishing Co. Limited

Published in 1986 by
Stoddart Publishing Co. Limited

Reprinted in 1989 by
Stoddart Publishing Co. Limited

Revised editions published in 1998 & 2005 by
Harold Taylor Time Consultants Inc.
1-800-361-8463

_____

CANADIAN CATALOGUING IN PUBLICATION DATA

Taylor, Harold L.
        Making time work for you: a guide to productive time
management

Rev. ed.
Includes index
ISBN 0-9683670-0-3

1. Executives – Time Management. I. Title.

HD69.T54T395 1998   658.4'093   C98-931192-9

Printed in Canada

Dedication

To my friends in the
National Association of Professional Organizers
who are a constant encouragement
and inspiration.

TABLE OF CONTENTS

INTRODUCTION

1. DEVELOP A TIME MANAGEMENT PHILOSOPHY

The real value of time. The secret of managing yourself effectively with respect to time. The necessity of personal goals and mission statements. How to make room for those important activities in your life. Time management myths.

2. GET RID OF THE BACKLOG

The Disorganized Desk Test. Taking the first step in managing yourself with respect to time. How to get rid of the backlog. How to clear your desk and keep on top of current paperwork. The 6 D's of mail handling. The follow-up file.

3. DEVELOP A TIME POLICY

Using your prime time. Time policy chart. Scheduling a "quiet hour." Deciding how to spend your day. How to divide your day into time segments devoted to specific tasks. How to utilize each hour most effectively.

4. SCHEDULE YOUR ACTIVITIES

The "to do" list fallacy. How to schedule your activities using a planning calendar. Selecting a planner that works for you. Scheduling priorities and personal time. How planning helps you say no. /50

5.   TIME MANAGEMENT WITH AN ELECTRONIC HANDHELD COMPUTER
The Palm as a Personal Organizer. The paper planner versus the PDA. Using a PDA for planning. Organizing your electronic *to do* list. A great traveling companion. The alarming side of the Palm. PDAs require manual labor. /64

6.   ORGANIZE YOURSELF AND YOUR OFFICE
Making your environment work for you. How to arrange your desk, files and furniture for maximum efficiency. Developing effective work habits. The use of binders. The alpha-numerical file system. Electronic filing. Hints for effective filing. /82

7.   ADD STRUCTURE TO YOUR LIFE
How to develop a Personal Organizer. The Telephone & Visitor's Log, Delegation Record, Meeting Participant's Action Sheet, Telephone Directory and other forms that will add structure to your life. The importance of writing things down. /98

8.   SLAY THE PAPERWORK DRAGON
Declare war on paperwork. Trimming the fat from your files. The tyranny of the in-basket. Coping with the magazine explosion. Reading smarter. How to

write brief, effective business letters and reports. Searching the Internet.

9. WRITING, SENDING AND RECEIVING EFFECTIVE E-MAIL

Advantages and disadvantages of e-mail. Managing e-mail: sending and receiving. Schedule time for e-mail. Keeping e-mail to a minimum. Don't hide behind e-mail. The evolution of Spam.

10   THE ENEMIES OF TIME MANAGEMENT

Your major timewaster. How to change the procrastination habit to the "do it now" habit. Overcoming absentmindedness and perfectionism. How to increase your level of awareness.

11.   DELEGATE FOR RESULTS

Extending the results you can achieve. Determining the activities to eliminate, delegate, or do yourself. How to delegate effectively and develop your employees. The principles of delegation. The Pareto Principle in action.

12. COPING WITH STRESS

Control your reaction to stress. Don't let hassles get you down. Managing your health. Avoiding burnout. The power of laughter. The major causes of stress. Tips for handling stress.

13.   DON'T FALL INTO THE MEETING TRAP

The high cost of meetings. How to reduce the time spent in meetings. How to ensure adequate preparation and follow-up. Maintaining control. Making meetings more productive. Time-saving tips for meeings.

14. MAKE THE MOST OF BUSINESS TRIPS

Managing your travel time while in the air and on the road. How to utilize all your travel time to your advantage. How to use checklists and your office in a briefcase. Travel tips for frequent flyers. How technology can save time. Cellular telephones.

15.   DON'T LET OTHERS STEAL YOUR TIME

How to control interruptions. Handling drop-in visitors and telephone calls. Managing your voice mail and e-mail. Making crises a learning experience. Know when to say no.

16. HELP EMPLOYEES MANAGE THEIR TIME

How employees waste time. Making time management a team effort. How to stop wasting your employees' time. How to encourage them to manage their own time effectively. How your assistant can help. Efficiency vs. effectiveness. Motivation through delegation. Provide computer training. /254

17. TIME MANAGEMENT IN THE HOME

How to apply time management techniques in the home. Making up a family organizer. Storage systems. Keeping the household organized. Are you sleeping too much? Time-saving strategies for home use. Fighting the packrat syndrome. /268

18. MAKE TIME MANAGEMENT A WAY OF LIFE

Developing self-discipline. How to form the time management habit. How to insure continued use of time management techniques. Keeping a time log. Twenty-five keys to effective time management. Keeping balance in your life. /280

LIST OF EXHIBITS

Introduction

I assume you have already read at least one or two of the hundreds of books that have been published on time management. I also assume, that after having read them, you are still unable to accomplish what you would like to accomplish in the time at your disposal. I think it's a safe assumption to make. Otherwise you wouldn't have picked up yet another book on time management.

What's the problem? Well, it may be that you're disorganized. If so, shaving an hour a day from your normal activities will not help because the remaining activities will simply expand to fill the extra time that you have available. Good old *Parkinson's Law!* If that's the case, no seminar, course, or book will solve your problem. If you're disorganized to start with, you'll be disorganized afterwards. If you have sloppy, inconsistent work habits, a poorly laid out office, a cluttered work environment, inadequate file systems, then tips on time management will be of little value. The few minutes shaved from telephone conversations, meetings or other activities won't mean a thing.

But if you will spend a few hours with me reading the following pages and following the suggestions, you will be able to develop effective work habits, organize your office, files and methods, and streamline your workflow. In short, you will be able to get organized. *You will be able to manage yourself effectively with respect to time.*

That's what it's all about. Forget about other people. *They're* not your problem. You can't change other people if they don't want to be changed. Nor can you manage time. Time is perfectly managed by itself. One hour follows the next in perfect symmetry. What you can and should manage is *yourself.* Read this book slowly. Try out the suggestions as they appear. They'll get you organized. Just as they've helped organize thousands of others who have attended my seminars and workshops. You may never have to read another book on time management.

In the original edition, published in 1981 by Stoddart Publishing [formerly General Publishing] there was little mention of technology of any kind, whether it be voice mail, e-mail, computer technology or the Internet. In this revised edition, they are covered, including new ideas that I have been able to put into practice since writing the original book twenty-five years ago. But technology continues to evolve and many ideas become obsolete quickly. Don't let it bother you if you see a reference to a Palm V for example, when the current offering is a Treo 680 or a MIlennium 300. The principles stil apply. One thing has *not* changed, and that is the value of time. It seems to be more precious now than ever before. Follow along with me as I demonstrate how you can free up more of this precious commodity called time, so that it can be used to enrich your life.

Harold Taylor
September, 2005

Chapter 1: Develop a time management philosophy

The true value of time

The value of time, like most commodities, is determined by supply and demand. If oil were in ample supply, it would not be as expensive. Similarly, water is considered to be inexpensive by most of us; but to someone lost in the desert, it is worth a fortune.

Time is the most valuable commodity of all. It is a non-renewable resource. Scientists will never be able to find a substitute. When our time is gone, *we're* gone.

Time seems to pass quickly for some, more slowly for others. For time is measured in past accomplishments. Those who look back and see few goals accomplished, few achievements, few times when they felt proud of what they have done - those people feel that life has sped by too quickly. They feel cheated. But those who look back and are flooded with memory after memory of satisfying activities, achievements, relationships, feel they have lived a long and fruitful life.

For time is not seen as minutes, hours, or days. You can't see intangibles that have no substance. Time is seen as events. Happenings. Experiences. It's seen as the glow on your children's faces when you tell them you are taking them to the zoo on Saturday. It's seen as the applauding crowd when you end your address to the home and school association. It's seen as the first check you receive for a short story submitted to a magazine. It's seen as that first promotion. It's seen as the pile of congratulatory cards when you graduate from college. Time is measured in events, not seconds. Squander time, and there will be fewer events to recall. Fewer accomplishments. Fewer moments of happiness. Squander time, and you squander life.

If you are business-oriented you probably calculate time's value by determining your hourly rate, applying a percentage for overhead and emerging with a figure of, let's say, $52 per hour. Then you attempt to motivate yourself to stop wasting time by telling yourself that for each hour wasted you are throwing away $52. That's the way many time management experts approach it.

Unfortunately it seldom works. Most people are spendthrifts. They know the value of money and yet still squander it. After all, money can be replaced. Give us time and we can always earn more money.

There's the paradox. Time is *not* money. We need time to *earn* money. Time is *increments of life.* We can use life for anything, but if it's all used up earning money, what else will there be to remember?

Do you want to spend the rest of your life earning money? Do you want your life to speed by with only memories of the activity of work? Or do you want to look back years from now and see the accomplishments, the achievements, the rewards? If you do, you had better start managing your life right now. You won't get a second chance.

There's no time to manage time

"I've just got to delegate more. I'm running like crazy from morning till night," confesses one manager. "But I just don't have the time to train anyone." "I know we need written procedures," relates another. "Every time someone is sick, we're in a mess. But who has the time to sit down and write procedures? Certainly not me!" "Sure, that's a great follow-up system. And I like the idea of a *Telephone and Visitors Log*. That's fine if you've got the time to set it up!" "I've finally made one of your time management seminars. This is the third time I've registered. Twice before I had to cancel out. I'm just too busy." These are actual comments made at some of my time management seminars. And they're typical. *We just don't have time to manage our time.* And it's true. If we *did* have time to manage our time we'd have no need to manage it.

That's why most people fail in their attempts to manage time. Because they are so busy, they grab at the little time savers contained in books and articles: "How to cut three minutes off your telephone time" or "Ten ways to save time at meetings." They shy away from the more extensive suggestions such as "get organized" or "delegate" or "design your own systems," because these are time consuming tasks in themselves. And time is the one thing that they lack.

Unfortunately, it is impossible to manage time. Time will be the same after we've left this earth as it was before we came. Time is unchangeable. Inflexible. Unyielding. No matter how you measure it, how you describe it, or how you use it, time cannot be influenced by any person on this earth. All we can ever hope to do is to *manage ourselves with respect to time.* To do this it does *not* take more time. It can't. Because there *is* no more time. It's all being used up. It's impossible *not* to use it, whether it be for sleeping, working, or day-dreaming.

Whenever we want to perform some task that we are not presently doing, we have to displace other activities to make room for it. And therein lies the secret of what is referred to as effective time management. *To be effective we must displace less important tasks with more important ones.* We can't wait until we have time to take on another task. We will never have any more time than we have right now. What we have to do is free up some of the time we have by eliminating non-productive or low priority activities and quickly replacing them with more valuable activities. Our effectiveness as managers is determined by the ratio of productive vs. non-productive activities filling the time at our disposal. And remember, *all* time is at our disposal.

Now take a look at those methods of managing ourselves with respect to time: the organized desk and work environment; the streamlined filing systems and follow-up files; the practice of delegation; the use of forms, logs, checklists; the written procedures; the planning and scheduling of activities; and the dozens of sensible suggestions found in some of the time management books, articles, and seminars - the suggestions that you have been putting off because you don't have the time to apply them.

Well you *have* the time. It's being utilized on activities that can be eliminated. *Believe* it. Everything you *do* can be eliminated. Some are vital to life and health so you won't want to eliminate them. Others are vital to your family and social life and you will not want to eliminate those. But all the activities you do during your 8 or 9 hours at work *can* be eliminated (at least temporarily) without the world collapsing. Or even the business. If not, heaven help your business if you ever take a week's vacation, get sick for a few days, or get caught in traffic one morning.

There is nothing more vital to your success as a manager than managing yourself effectively with respect to time. When you are managing yourself effectively, you are getting more accomplished. Not in less time. There's no such thing as more time or less time. But you are getting more things accomplished. *Meaningful things that move you closer to your personal and organizational goals.*

You don't have the time to manage your time? Well listen, you've got all the time there is to have. And the longer you procrastinate, the less you'll get out of life. So make a decision *now* to start managing yourself with respect to time.

What is important to you?

Before you can start eliminating or condensing the unimportant activities in your life, you must have a clear understanding of what the *important* activities are. *What is important to you?* What do you want to accomplish during your lifetime? You need to know. That's what time management (life management) is all about. *The accomplishment of significant goals at the expense of those unimportant, time consuming activities.*

If you've never thought about it before, now's the time to start. Plan your future. Visualize the type of person you want to be; what goals you want to achieve. Goals add purpose to life. They give us direction. Without them we drift, easy prey to the hundreds of time wasting activities that plague us all.

Your goals must be in writing. Don't kid yourself into believing that those nebulous thoughts about what you want to do next year or the year after are actually goals. They aren't. They're nebulous thoughts. Goals are in writing with deadline dates and a plan of action for achieving them. They must be specific and measurable. Make sure your goals don't conflict with one another. It's unlikely you'll be able to save $20,000 and take a trip around the world in the same year. Make sure your goals are realistic.

Separate your goals into personal, family, and business goals. Here again, there should be no conflict. If you want to become president of the company, write a best-selling novel, and spend two hours every night with your family, there may indeed be conflict. Decide which goal is most important to you and give it priority.

For each goal, write down a list of steps necessary to accomplish it. These steps will then become the activities you will use to replace the unimportant activities now being pursued. If you feel threatened by the goal-setting process, or are not sure how to start, refer to my book, *Say Yes To Your Dreams* [Harold Taylor Time Consultants Inc., 1998.]

Determine your mission

Most of the people who have a clear set of tangible personal goals, have never really taken the time to examine their mission in life. A failure to examine your values first may result in goals that are at cross-purposes to them. Discomfort, stress, and feelings of guilt may ensue. If your pursuits are in harmony with your values you will be happy - at peace with yourself.

The number of values is unlimited and will vary from person to person. Home life is a value. Doing God's will is a value. Fame is a value. Materialism, self-reliance, sincerity, freedom, career, friendship, health, morality are all values. Participate in a brainstorming session alone or with a partner. Write down all the things that you feel is important to you. Values are things we consider worthwhile - our personal standards.

They establish our sense of purpose and direction. Writing them down ensures that we are able to express them, understand them, and become committed to them. We may think we know what we want; but thoughts are fleeting. Words on paper are more concrete.

Once our beliefs are on paper, we can evaluate them, change them, and make them adequately express where we stand as individuals. Keep that mission statement handy as you formulate your goals. Reconsider any goals that seem to conflict with your values. The result should be a set of goals that are consistent with your purpose in life. They will be much easier to achieve. And a lot more enjoyable. Your personal mission is not your vocation, it *determines* your vocation. Nor is it the same as your company's mission, although it should be compatible. My personal mission, for example, is *To help others organize their lives by sharing ideas through books, seminars and by personal example so they are free to do the work God has given them to do.* It would be difficult for me to fulfill my mission by working in a factory or an office. But it could be fulfilled in an educational environment or as a consultant, speaker, or writer.

If your mission is compatible with your work, you will be more motivated, experience less stress, become more effective and find greater fulfillment in the performance of your job. Goals describe what you will do, how you will do it, and when you will do it. A mission explains *why* you do it. As Richard J. Leider said in his book, *The Power Of Purpose*, "The way to spend our precious time and energy wisely is to know the purpose for which we live and then to deliberately organize our lives accordingly."

Time management is a reachable goal for those who have the motivation. But you must see time as it really is, as a measure of your life. You must know what you want to accomplish during your lifetime, the things that are really important to you. Then you will succeed because you will be able to displace those relatively unimportant activities with the more meaningful activities - activities which will lead you to your goals.

You can do it. Resolve now that you will respect every hour as a piece of your life. I will show you how to eliminate those activities that are unnecessary. And how to condense those activities that are necessary but unworthy of the slice of your life they are consuming. Then you can use the resulting free time for meaningful activities that will lead you to your lifetime goals.

Time management myths

Before I proceed, I want to dispel some common myths that seem to permeate time management books and literature.

Myth # 1. *We can manage time.* As I already stated, we cannot manage time. Nor can we save it. Time ticks away relentlessly in spite of our efforts to control it. We are provided with 24 hours of time each day to use as we like. The key is in how we use that time. We can use it wisely, or we can waste it, but we can never save it. At the end of the day, it's gone.

Myth # 2. *Time management is getting more done in less time.* This may be a *result* of time management; but it is not the *essence* of time management. The essence of time management is doing fewer things of greater importance in the time that we have. We cannot possibly do everything we *want* to do, nor all the things there *are* to do. But if we prioritize our tasks and focus on completing the priorities to the exclusion of everything else, we will be more effective. Don't do *more* things; do *more important* things.

Myth # 3. *"To do" lists help get things done.* "To do" lists do nothing to further a project or task. They simply remind us that they are not done yet. Scheduling time in your planner, as appointments with yourself, and then working on those tasks gets them done. "To do" lists are intentions; scheduled blocks of time are commitments. "To do" lists should only be used for the routine, relatively unimportant tasks that you plan to get done.

Myth # 4. *People need a "Personal Organizer" to get organized.* People are not organized because they use a time management system, they use a time management system because they are organized. Personal organization involves breaking old habits and forming new, effective ones. It is a state of mind as opposed to a state of the office. Some people are more organized using a 65 cent steno pad than others are using a 65 dollar organizer. So get organized first, then use an organizer. Once you are organized, tools such as a Personal Organizer will definitely help keep you on track.

Myth # 5. *A "Quiet Hour" is a great time management tool.* A "quiet hour" is a figment of time management writers' imaginations. There is really no such thing as a perfect "quiet hour". We can *reduce* interruptions, but never eliminate them. To be effective we must learn to work in *spite* of the interruptions. Frequently, interruptions are not time wasters, but opportunities arriving at inopportune times. Having said that, we should make every attempt to reduce interruptions while we work on priority tasks. It is in this context that I use the term "quiet hour" in this book. But don't expect it to be interruption-free.

Myth # 6. *Keeping a time log to determine where your time is going is the place to start.* A time log should be done last, not first. All we need is more paperwork and interruptions when we're already inundated with them! We should get organized first, adopt effective habits, schedule time properly, put into practice time-reducing techniques and procedures. Then and only then should we keep a time log to effect further refinements.

Myth # 7. *The biggest time wasters include telephone interruptions, visitors, meetings and rush jobs.* These are not time wasters, they are time *obligations* ; they come with the job. The biggest time wasters are self-imposed, such as procrastination, making mental notes, interrupting ourselves, searching for things, perfectionism, and spending time on trivial tasks. We are our own worst enemies. Being effective involves *managing ourselves*, not placing the blame on others.

Myth # 8. *It's more efficient to stick to one task until it's completed.* It may be more efficient, but it's not more effective, for some of the tasks may never get done. It's more effective to break large projects into small one or two-hour chunks and work at them for brief periods each day. Working on priorities involves frequent brief sprints, not occasional marathons.

Myth # 9. *We should have one planner for the office, and a separate planner for the home.* We should have one planner, period. We are only one person, sharing our lives with people and activities at work, at home, at school, etc. Since we only have one life, we should only have one planner. Both business and personal activities should be scheduled in the same planner so business activities don't take precedence over personal and family activities. If your planner is electronic and its use dictated by the company, it may be necessary to keep it synched with a PDA to keep it portable.

Myth #10. *Time is money.* As already discussed, time is more than money, it's life. You can always get more money, but you can never get more time. It's an irreplaceable resource. When time's gone, you're gone. We must never lose our respect for time.

Chapter 2

Get rid of the backlog

Clean up the mess

You arrive at the office in time to be handed yet another bulging file of papers for approval. The stack of magazines on your credenza has grown higher. The phone messages on your spike have multiplied. Yesterday's unanswered mail is buried beneath the latest arrivals. Unfinished projects are barely visible beneath the clutter of memos, messages, and miscellaneous material. You haven't touched your e-mail for two days. The phone rings. You pick it up, while gesturing to the two employees who have followed you into your office. They wait patiently with their problems while you hastily generate yet another scrap of paper while confirming to the caller that you will "look into it right away."

Hold everything! Hang up the phone, chase out those employees, and lock the office door. Don't risk ulcers or become another heart-attack statistic. Remember, it's your life you're wasting with these meaningless activities. Searching through piles of papers and hopping from crisis to crisis is not your bag. You have too much respect for your time and too many goals that you want to accomplish. If you're not sure whether your desk is considered a disaster area, take the following test.

The disorganized desk test

❑ Most of the paperwork on my desk is stacked horizontally.

❑ My in-basket is on my desk.

❏ My telephone is on my desk.

❏ I spend at least ten minutes most days looking for things on my desk.

❏ There is a stack of magazines or other reading material on my desk most of the time.

❏ Other people are reluctant to leave paperwork on my desk for fear it might get lost.

❏ At least one person during the past week left something on my chair or on top of a project I was working on so I'd be sure to see it.

❏ It is difficult for other people to find a document on my desk if I'm not there.

❏ At any one time there are at least three unfinished projects lying on my desk.

❏ My desk is usually messy when I leave at night.

❏ In addition to paperwork, I keep at least five other items on my desk [e.g.: stapler, pencil caddie, paper-clip holder, calendar, rubber bands, tape, ink stamp, cup, bookends, photographs, books.]

❏ During most of the day you can see very little of my desk top - over 75 percent is covered with files, paperwork.

❑ Some days I have paper arranged on the floor adjacent to my desk while working.

❑ I have more than one "junk drawer" in my desk.

❑ A ledge under my desk, a window sill or the top of a filing cabinet is being used to store paperwork, at least temporarily.

❑ During a typical week, several people comment on the state of my desk top.

❑ There is not enough room in my filing cabinet to house the paperwork on my desk.

❑ Every week, at least two people ask me about the status of a memo or report that has been given to me for action.

❑ I make notes on scraps of paper which frequently get lost or misplaced.

❑ I sometimes move to another desk or table so I'll have room to work.

Scoring

0 to 4 True: You are above average in your organizing skills, and are probably experiencing a high level of productivity.

5 to 10 True: You will never win a "messiest desk"

award, but your personal productivity is likely being hampered.

10 to 15 True: Chances are, you are spending a lot of time searching for things, shuffling paper, and becoming distracted. Your productivity is suffering as a result.

15 to 20 True: Your desk is a conversation piece and is affecting other people's productivity as well. Take action before it's declared a disaster area.

Any score over 4 warrants a reassessment of your work area.

Your first step in making room for important activities which will lead you to your goals is to get rid of the backlog of paperwork and other obligations which precipitate interruptions and crises, and sap your energy.

Your priority task *right now* is to clear your desk and in-basket. If you're not organized, if you don't quickly stem the flow of paperwork and communications, you'll be bogged down again in no time. You have to start with the ruthless decision to barricade your door, have your calls intercepted, and be "out" to all visitors for at least a half-day. If you feel guilty about this due to all those urgent matters that need attending to, reflect for a moment on what would happen if you actually *were* out -with a bad case of ulcers, a nervous breakdown, or worse. If you're still convinced it's impossible, dedicate a Saturday or a day of your vacation to the task. It's worth it.

Before you set up procedures which will keep you organized, you have to clean up the mess. And this is no time for neatness. Grab four envelope boxes. Mark them "Magazines", "Junk Mail", "Routine", and "Priority". Toss all magazines into one. Throw all junk mail into another. Clear that desk. Low priority items go into the third carton marked "Routine". Top priority items go into the last one. Don't waste too much time determining the difference. If in doubt, it goes into the low priority carton. At this stage, consider priority items to be those that relate directly to your goals. *They could be either urgent or not urgent; but they must all be important.* Within a half hour you should have your desk and credenza tops completely cleared. If it takes longer, you're actually reading the paperwork or thinking about it, or setting especially significant items aside. Don't fall into this trap or you'll sidetrack yourself to death.

It's a wonderful feeling to have a clear desk, but don't waste time contemplating it. Take that priority carton and start dispensing with the items one at a time. Don't pick from beneath the pile. Deal with the top item first, then the second and so on. Spend a good two hours on this top priority carton. Some may be easy, requiring only a hastily scribbled note of instruction to your assistant, a handwritten reply, or a simple "please handle" notation as you set it in the outgoing pile. Others may require twenty minutes or more of your time, several phone calls and some e-mail. But do it. You may encounter an item that takes you a full hour or more to complete. Block off time in your planner to do it and place the paperwork in a follow-up file.

When you've sorted your backlog of paperwork and spent at least two hours dispensing with priority items, it's time to plan a tentative schedule for the balance of the week - to be reviewed and changed later as you see

Exhibit 1

Follow-up File

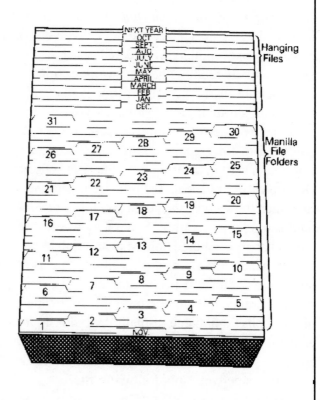

fit. For the first week you may want to spend an hour or more each morning on that top-priority carton, moving to the low priority one when it's completed. During this period have your assistant intercept your phone calls and visitors, and guard your closed door. If you have no assistant, at least close your door, engage your voice mail, and deal with all interruptions as quickly as possible. Don't allow yourself to get sidetracked during that first hour each morning. To get organized properly you *must* start with a clear desk. The psychological lift it will give you will propel you through the subsequent stages of managing yourself with respect to time. After one or two weeks your entire backlog of work in those cartons will disappear. Your hour in the morning can then be devoted to going through those cartons of junk mail and magazines.

Don't spend much time on them. And don't be tempted to keep anything unless you can foresee a profitable use for it. Skim the magazines quickly. Tear out any articles you may want to refer to later during leisure hours, and get rid of the magazines. Never thumb through pages twice. In Chapter 7 you will learn how to easily cope with a constant barrage of books, magazines, and reports; but in the meantime, just get rid of them quickly. Even if you have to pass them on or throw them out unread. Never let that desk get cluttered again. Whatever your scheduled time is for incoming mail, stick to it. Pick up each piece of paper only once. Follow the *6 D's of mail handling*:

The 6 D's of mail handling

Discard it. If you can do without it, get rid of it. Send it to the recycle bin or to the trash can. This refers to junk mail or one-way communications that simply say, "thank you," "for your information," or "please note." Destroy it. Ditch it. Don't keep it if you don't have to.

Delegate it. If it's something that must be acted upon, and it can be done by somebody else who earns less salary than you do, delegate it. You cannot afford to pay $100/hour labor for $30/hour work. Designate a due date and direct it to a member of your staff. Record the due date in the "Follow-up" section of your planner.

Do it. If it must be done, and you're the only one who can do it, and it will take ten minutes or less, do it now. Don't defer it, dodge it or disown it. Dig in and do it. It could be a quick telephone call to reply to a letter, or an e-mail message, or a brief report. Dispense with it quickly. Don't drag it out.

Develop it. If it's important, can only be done by yourself, and will take longer than ten minutes, determine *when* you will do it, and schedule that time in your planner. Develop an action plan now that will ensure that it gets done in time, regardless of its magnitude. Even if the task will take 100 hours, schedule the first few hours this week. When the two hours are over, schedule another few hours the following week and so on until it's completed. How many blocks of time you schedule each week is determined by the deadline date of the task. Don't put it on a "To Do" list if it's a priority. If you're serious about doing it, schedule time to do it. Put the paperwork in a follow-up file corresponding to the date you have it scheduled.

Delay it. If it should be done, can only be done by you, but is not a priority, delay it by adding it to your "Things To Do" list. Work at it during spare moments that week; but don't spend prime time on it. And don't let it displace the important tasks. If it *never* gets done, it's no big deal. The paperwork can go into a "To Do" folder in your right hand drawer or in a step file on your desk.

Deposit it. If the paperwork is informational and must be retained for future reference, drop it in your filing system or deposit it in a 3-ring binder so you can retrieve it easily. Don't toss it aside with the intention of filing it later.

Develop the *do it now* habit when dealing with paperwork. By following the "6 D" formula for dispensing with paperwork you are handling paper a minimum number of times. You either discard it, delegate it, do it, develop it, delay it or deposit it. Double handling will decrease, distractions will desist, and disorganization will disappear.

Keep your desk clear

Once you are rid of the backlog of work, you have to organize the flow of paperwork so it doesn't get ahead of you again. If someone opens your mail don't let them throw everything together. Have one folder for top priority items, a second for routine matters, and a third one for junk mail. (If you prefer, you can have your assistant screen the junk mail. Personally, I get a lot of good ideas from these unsolicited items, and like to browse through them quickly after completing my routine mail.) Have each folder a different color for easy identification.

Magazines should be separate. Your mail should come to you with the top priority file on top. And that's where you start. If you can resist the overwhelming urge to peek beneath the piles, I guarantee you've got what it takes to manage yourself successfully.

If you cannot start on something because the information required hasn't arrived yet, or it's too soon to take action, get it off your desk and into a follow-up file. Pick a time each day to work on your incoming mail. Try to stick to this routine. If there is no one to sort your mail, simply use the 6 D's of mail handling and handle each piece of paper only once.

The follow-up file

A clear desk does not guarantee that you'll be organized. But it helps. If you have a handful of material relating to a project and nowhere to put it, don't leave it on your desk or toss it back into the in-basket. Develop a follow-up file. This follow-up file is exclusive of your assistant's. If your assistant keeps a follow-up file and uses it to jog your memory or return letters, reports, etc. to you for follow-up or approval, that's great. But this is your personal follow-up file which contains the back-up material for those tasks that you have scheduled in your time planner. Nothing goes into this follow-up file unless a time to complete it has been blocked off in your planning calendar, or, in the case of simple reminders, a note jotted in the follow-up section of your planner.

The follow-up file system consists of thirteen hanging files marked January, February, etc., and the last one marked "next year." One set of manila folders marked from 1 to 31, corresponding to the days of the month is placed in the current month's hanging folder. One set only, not one set for every month. You may need a few unmarked hanging folders for the current month in order to accommodate all these manila folders. If it's the first of the month and you have emptied the day's project papers, move the manila folder to the next month's hanging folder. This allows you to have 31 days ahead of you at all times.

This follow-up file system is simply an adjunct to your time planner. Your planner contains your work plan. When you arrive in the morning, flip open your time planner and see a report scheduled for 9:00 a.m., you know exactly where to look for the back-up papers needed, in that day's follow-up file.

If more papers are received related to a specific task that is scheduled for a future date, it's a simple matter to find the appropriate follow-up file folder. Simply flip through your time planner to find the date on which that project is scheduled.

For on-going projects such as committee meetings, book manuscripts, and bulky engineering projects, it's not necessary (or advisable) to jam all the back-up material into the follow-up folders. Instead, use a colored manila folder bearing the project's name or title. Keep them in your right hand desk drawer, along with your follow-up file. Use hanging folders for these project files for easy retrieval. You will soon know at a glance that the red folder is "A" project, the green folder the "B" project, and so on.

Never do anything if you can delegate it, never delegate it if you can scrap it, and never file anything permanently unless it's vital that you refer to it again in the future.

For outgoing mail, set up a tier of out-baskets bearing the names of your employees and those who inter-rupt you on a regular basis. Anything you can possibly delegate should be sorted quickly and placed in these baskets with your instructions. Have others pick up their paperwork whenever they interrupt you. Even your boss's memos don't have to be delivered if he or she is in the habit of dropping in a few times each day.

Guard your time carefully. It's your most valuable resource, so don't let others steal it. So far you've been able to clear up your backlog of paperwork, streamline the flow, keep a clear desk, and keep on top of current paperwork. You have forced yourself to work on priori-ty items first, and all in all you feel a little better organ-ized. But it's only temporary. Unless you set a daily time schedule - and stick to it - you'll be buried beneath paperwork again in no time.

In the next chapter, I'll show you how to develop a policy on time utilization which will keep your desk clear and prevent you from being victimized by external time bandits.

Chapter 3

Develop a time policy

Don't give away your prime time

It's 8:45 a.m.. and a cheery "good morning" echoes throughout the office as you make your way to your desk. You feel great. You always feel great first thing in the morning. You're what people refer to as a "morning person." Energy is at its peak from the time you swing out of bed at 6:00 a.m. until your enthusiasm takes a nose-dive just before noon.

"Oh, say," a voice follows you into your office, "could you approve these overtime slips and sign the payroll checks when you get a minute?"

"Might as well get it over with now," you mutter in response, vaguely recalling a *do it now* principle expounded in a recent article on time management. "Hang on a minute, Alice." Alice hangs on while you hastily scratch your signature on form after form. Alice gets tired of hanging on and disappears. Other shadows replace her.

"Can I talk to you while you're signing those things?" one of the shadows asks. "I want to get your opinion on these new accounts."

"Sure, talk away," you offer, only half listening. Other shadows drop papers on your desk as you finish signing the checks. The telephone rings. You hastily close the discussion on the new accounts as you reach for the phone. More visitors. Morning mail. Faxes. E-mail. Voice mail messages. Your enthusiasm wanes. You decide on an early coffee break. But it's not that early. Nearly two hours have slipped away. "What a waste," you admonish yourself. "I haven't accomplished a thing yet and I have to leave in an hour for my luncheon appointment."

What a waste indeed. Not only have you not accomplished anything of consequence, but you have squandered the most valuable part of your day - your prime time. If you are indeed a "morning person", you owe it to yourself to schedule your quiet hour during this early morning period. Close your door. Have phone calls and visitors intercepted. Don't schedule appointments or make outgoing calls during this time. Instead, spend the time and that abundance of energy working on your priority task, the task which will have the greatest impact on the accomplishment of your personal and organizational goals.

Many of us feel guilty about being inaccessible to others. We think it is our duty to be available at all times, to have an "open door policy." And yet we would never think of allowing interruptions when we are in conference with our employees, clients, or customers. We view it as rude to talk on the telephone, receive visitors, or be inattentive in such situations.

If we don't feel guilty about respecting other people's time, why should we feel guilty about respecting our own? We have just as much right (if not more) to hold meetings with ourselves. In fact we owe it both to ourselves and to our companies. Only by scheduling interruption-free time each day can we maximize our effectiveness as managers. Almost everyone will agree that they can get twice as much done in an hour of uninterrupted time (and do it better) than they can in two hours under normal office conditions. And no wonder. It is estimated that the average executive is interrupted every 8 minutes. How can we possibly be effective when we have to stop a job and reorient ourselves every 8 minutes! Let's do what we can to reduce both the frequency and duration of these interruptions.

Use your prime time wisely

This "quiet hour" should coincide with the time of the day when your energy level is at its peak. For about 80 percent of the population, this is the first hour or two of the workday. For some it's late morning or late afternoon. When you feel wide awake, refreshed, enthusiastic, and mentally alert, that's the time you should schedule a meeting with yourself. Have as much respect for your own time as you have for other people's time.

Don't waste this precious prime time by working on mundane tasks such as reading magazines or cleaning out desk drawers. Utilize it for the tasks which are important, perhaps difficult. Ones that impact your goals. This could include planning, budgeting, working on a proposal for a new account or completing a major report which will affect you or your company's future.

If the hourly cost of your regular time works out to $50, then the hourly value of your prime time will be closer to $100. You just don't spend $100 to straighten a desk drawer, read newspapers, visit the copier machine, or discuss baseball scores with your co-workers. Avoid scheduling meetings with others during your prime time. Remember, it's more than money; it's part of your life that you're giving away.

If your prime time happens to be 8:30 a.m. to 10:00 a.m., then block out that time in your planner. Draw a box around that time slot most days for several weeks. Label them "meetings with yourself" or better still, jot down the name of the project you'll be working on. Then, when anyone asks "Can I see you first thing Thursday morning?" you look at your calendar and reply, "Well, I'm tied up until 10:00 a.m. Would 10 o'clock be okay? Don't let meetings, visitors or appointments pre-empt your quiet hour. If you do, you are not managing your time effectively. Admittedly, something will come up periodically that is even more important than the task you had scheduled for your quiet hour. If so, you have no choice but to pre-empt it. But this shouldn't happen very often. When it does, be aware of the cost. Car wash establishments, movie theaters, and certain other service companies, have additional charges for their prime time. Unless you're a consultant you can't very well place a premium on your prime time. But why give it away? Keep it for yourself and increase your effectiveness.

Some managers claim it's impossible to reserve a quiet hour on a regular basis. They agree it would be terrific, but then go on to say that they have to answer their own phone, or they don't have voice mail, or they don't have a private office, or the boss keeps interrupting them. Admittedly, these are all problems. But most problems have solutions. If all else fails, spend your quiet hour in another office, a boardroom, or at home. And, as far as the boss is concerned, I haven't met a boss yet who was not interested in increasing the productivity of his or her staff. That is, once the boss realized that the purpose of the quiet hour is to increase effectiveness, not to hide from more work. And effectiveness will increase if you use your time wisely. No quiet hour is perfectly quiet. There will be interruptions that you can't ignore. But you allow for these when scheduling work sessions. The "how to's" of scheduling will be covered in chapter 4.

Your time policy

Since you will never be able to get any more time than

you already have, being effective becomes a matter of using your time wisely. It involves planning weeks or months ahead. It involves realistic estimates of how long each task will take. It involves self-discipline, concentration, and the power to resist distractions. And, above all, it involve developing a time policy. You have already carved out a period of time for a quiet hour. It's your policy to spend this prime time on priority work. But now you should formulate a time policy covering your entire day.

A time policy is a guide to be used in scheduling your tasks, appointments, meetings and other activities. It involves reserving certain periods of the day for specific activities. This makes you more effective in several ways. The habit (as it eventually becomes) of performing the same types of tasks at the same time each day reduces the brain's "start-up time" - the time it normally takes to get itself in gear and oriented to the task. It also allows you to make use of the natural breaks in a day (coffee breaks, lunch, quitting time) as deadlines to prevent jobs expanding to fill a greater time span (Parkinson's Law). This is particularly helpful in the case of meetings or appointments which tend to take twice as long as they should. And, of course, a time policy ensures that you use your prime time effectively - for priority tasks - leaving those routine activities for the afternoon doldrums.

I'm a "morning person" myself. I can get as much done before 10:00 a.m. as I can the rest of the day. Therefore, I guard this prime time jealously. If you don't make it a policy to utilize your prime time working on priority tasks, you'll find yourself scheduling appointments, meetings, sorting through e-mail or making calls during this most valuable part of your day. If your prime time happens to be in the late afternoon or mid-morning, fine. Set your priority tasks and quiet hour to coincide with that particular time. Your policy should be not to return phone calls, visitors, or work on routine tasks during this prime time.

Next, perhaps you would like to set a policy to hold all your staff meetings, interviews, counseling etc. late in the afternoon, let's say 4:00 to 5:00 p.m., as indicated on the time policy chart in Exhibit 2. This would be a particularly good time to hold meetings since they tend to end a lot sooner with 5:00 o'clock threatening. This would also be a good time to hand over all those assignments and tasks that you had thought of during the day. Resist the temptation to run back and forth between yourself and your employees handing out assignments as they occur to you. Instead, jot down the tasks you would like to delegate and add them to the list during the day. Then make one trip only - late in the afternoon. Interrupt your employees only once and you'll avoid wasting their time as well as your own.

Now you may want to set a policy of completing your routine tasks during the afternoon hours when your energy level has decreased and sluggishness has set in. This might be an excellent time to schedule visitors, return your telephone calls and work on those hundreds of "must do" items which do not require too much con-centration or thought.

You may want to set a policy of having lunch some-time between 12:00 and 1:30 p.m. You may decide to utilize the time left over from this lunch hour to review your voice mail and e-mail.

Important (but not priority) tasks, meetings, visitors,

e-mail and calls could be handled just subsequent to your prime time in that space between 10:30 a.m. and 12:00 noon. Here again is an excellent time to hold meetings, receive visitors and return calls, since conversations proceed more quickly with lunch hour only minutes away.

Once you have drawn up your own personal time policy chart, you should make your employees and associates aware of your policy concerning the scheduling of your time. Remember, this is only a policy. Policies are guidelines and can be changed if you have a very important visitor who insists upon seeing you in the morning (your boss, for instance). You may want to break your policy on occasion. But you will very quickly get into the habit of scheduling visitors, meetings, mail, magazines, etc. to fit your time policy chart.

The time policy chart

Let's take a look at the sample chart reproduced in Exhibit 2. This manager is in the habit of arriving about 8:30 a.m. Her policy is to spend that half hour reviewing voice mail, e-mail and faxes that accumulated overnight. It could also include checking her "idea" file in order to schedule some of them into her planner and a check of the follow up file. Some of the time might be spent simply reviewing the daily schedule and orienting herself to the tasks ahead.

Next comes her quiet hour between 9:00 a.m. and 10:30 a.m. during which time she starts working on previously scheduled priority tasks. This is the prime time which must be protected from interruptions. Her staff and business associates should be aware of the manager's unavailability during this time period. Calls should

Exhibit 2

Time Policy Chart

Voice mail, E-mail, faxes	8:30 am
	9:00 am
Quiet Hour Priority Tasks	
	10:30 am
Appointments Meetings Calls Correspondence	
	12 noon
Mail, Voice Mail, E-mail	
	12:30 pm
Exercise Lunch	
	2:00 pm
Appointments Priority Tasks	
	4:00 pm
Meetings Assignments Calls	
	5:00 pm

be screened or intercepted by voice mail and any essential interruptions kept to a minimum. This could be the most productive hour and a half of the manager's day.

From 10:30 AM. to 12:00 noon, she may have several visitors scheduled. She could also return calls during this period, meet with fellow employees, or simply work on routine tasks. Or, if time permits, continue with those priority tasks.

She would then handle her mail between 12:00 and 12:30 P.M. A little exercise, even though it might simply be a quick walk around the block, clears the cobwebs and increases efficiency during the afternoon. A light lunch could follow this exercise.

The next two hours or so would be spent dispensing with the bulk of those items on the "to do" list, making calls, completing projects, and in general working on tasks which do not require much energy. Finally, a meeting with her staff or a visit with some employees individually, developing assignments for the following day, rescheduling the tasks that are yet to be completed and planning the next day's schedule round out the afternoon.

You may have to experiment a little before formalizing your policy. Determine when you work best (your prime time) and when you feel sluggish. And review your scheduling policy every few months to see whether changing it might make you more effective.

If you have a secretary or assistant who makes your appointments for you, make sure he or she has a copy of your time policy chart. And don't allow deviations unless absolutely necessary. Give up your prime time grudgingly.

Chapter 4

Schedule your activities

"To do" list or not "to do" list

You're up to your elbows in a project that is taking longer than you thought and in the process of reaching for the phone to cancel a luncheon appointment, when one of your employees interrupts. "Got a minute?" he asks sheepishly. Of course you've got a minute. In fact, you've got 360 minutes before you have to pack your briefcase and join the five o'clock migration. What can you say? You've already been interrupted, so you might as well say "Sure, what is it?"

So you say it. And you half listen while squirming uncomfortably, eyes darting between the phone and the report you had been writing. After a few painful minutes he finally leaves with his partially answered question. But you know he'll be back. They always come back.

"There just isn't enough time in the day," you mutter to yourself. Don't you believe it. If there were more hours in a day you would simply have to endure the same situations over a longer period of time. There's no doubt you have a time problem. But the problem is not that you don't have enough time. It's how you're spending the time you've got.

You can't really schedule your time. That's already done for you. There are 24 hours in every day, 4:00 p.m. occurs at the same time each day, and 8:00 o'clock always follows 7:00 o'clock. But what you *can* and *should* do is to schedule your tasks. You must schedule your tasks in order to utilize your time effectively. And by scheduling I don't mean making a daily "to do" list. The practice of listing all the things you have to do and crossing them off as they're completed is better than nothing. Listing them in order of priority and working on the priority items first is a lot better. *But the most effective method is to schedule the priority tasks direct-ly into your planning calendar.*

I admit that some time management experts recommend that we spend time each morning (or the previous afternoon) writing a list of things to be done that day. But there's no way all those items could be done that day and, although they may claim that copying things over again "crystallizes our thinking," I believe it wastes our time. In fact, eventually we may convince our subconscious that the purpose of the exercise is to write out the jobs to be done rather than to do them. I've seen managers with a lengthy list headed "Things to do Today" when "today" was taken up with all day meetings or seminars. Others, who keep an ongoing "to do" list end up doing something that is not on their list. Would you believe it, they quickly add it on so they can cross it off!

Keep priority tasks off your "to do" list

Jobs, projects, reports, appraisal reviews - all the priority items of a "to do" list - should be scheduled in your planning calendar along with the meetings, appointments, and luncheon dates. Combine your "to do" list with your planning calendar and you have an actual schedule - a commitment - of when you will work on your important tasks. The real priority items of your "to do" list would appear this week on your calendar; the lower priority items might not appear for two or more weeks. But each task would be scheduled for a specific time on a specific day. If someone should ask if you're free for a meeting on Thursday afternoon at 3:00 p.m., the answer would be "no" if you had a report scheduled to be written at that time. Be sure to allow enough time for those priority tasks. A good rule is to allow at least 50% more time than you think it will take. This will compensate for those uncontrollable interruptions referred to earlier.

Don't schedule every hour of the week. Leave plenty of space for those urgent, priority crises that invariably occur. Typically I schedule about 25 percent to 30 percent of my week in advance. I fill the rest in as the week progresses.

Keep interruptions to a minimum. Since you are now treating your priority jobs as though they were meetings or appointments, you are justified in closing the door until that particular scheduled task has been completed. Look upon it as an appointment with yourself.

The important thing is to schedule your tasks. So get a functional planning calendar, preferably with a week-at-a-glance with a daily breakdown in half-hour units, and space for a weekly "to do" list. There are plenty on the market. I use one that I designed myself. It's called the Taylor Planner [See Exhibit 3.] and is available at our website, www.taylorintime.com.

The routine tasks should be broken down into weekly "to do" lists and recorded directly in your planning calendar - but as a list to one side, not in any particular time frame. These are items you peck away at during spare moments. If you misjudge the number of items you can accomplish in a week, you will still have to copy some onto the next week's schedule. Hopefully not many, for you have spread the items over several weeks. Although this is a "to do" list, note that it does

Exhibit 3

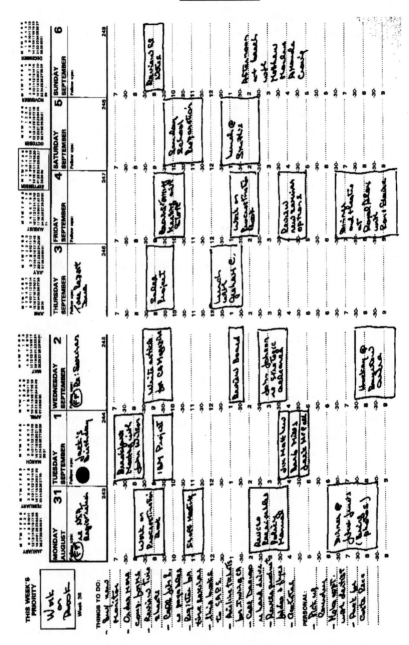

54

not contain any of the priority tasks.

How to select a planning calendar

A planner, diary, calendar, agenda or whatever you wish to call it, should do more than simply tell you what day it is. A planner should display your annual goals so you never lose sight of where you're heading and supply enough space to actually schedule time to work on those goal-related activities. It should also remind you of appointments, assignments due, meetings and special events such as birthdays, as well as list the multitude of things that you have to do that day or that week so you won't forget them. Finally, it should provide space for scheduling evening and weekend activities so your work won't crowd out personal commitments.

There are other things that planners could do for you. But don't choose a planner with all the bells and whistles if you never use bells and whistles. The planner should fit your personal management style, not the reverse. Some of the more analytical people prefer a day-at-a-glance, perhaps because they like detailed records of everything. Others prefer a month-at-a-glance because they're more interested in the overall picture and long-term results and don't want to get locked into the daily nitty gritty. I prefer the week-at-a-glance, so I can concentrate on detail, yet have an idea of how the week is shaping up. It provides space to schedule activities without the constant flipping of pages necessary in the day-at-a-glance planners. A. Roger Merrill, in his book *Connections: Quadrant II Time Management*, suggests that "the week is a complete little patch out of the fabric of life. It has the weekend, it has the evening, it has the workday." It's difficult to balance your life on a daily basis, but a weekly schedule puts things in perspective.

I recommend you use a larger planner as opposed to the pocket variety and schedule all activities and events; record all birthdays, anniversaries; describe all trips, vacations; include rough maps of how to get to places; list items to take to staff meetings and conferences, etc. Then your planning calendar will also serve as a record of where you have been and what you have done, complete with reusable information for the future. If you use a Palm or other PDA for your planning, you are limited in size; but you can still make it work as I will outline in the next chapter.

How to use your planner

More important than the planner you select is the way you use it. Keep your goals highlighted there, as well as your "to do" list, important telephone numbers, assignments due, commitments made, important events to remember and scheduled blocks of time for yourself. Don't be afraid to record information in your planner, including evening and weekend plans. People who simply use it as a calendar - to tell whether a holiday falls on a Monday or a Tuesday - are making a mistake. The more you use it the more valuable it becomes and the more organized you will be.

The *Taylor Planner* was designed to enable its user to continue to focus on priority goals throughout the year. There is a single page near the front of the planner for the current year's goals. List here those priority projects which you want to accomplish during the year. Not the routine jobs, only those key goals. If you don't have a goals page in your planner, you can easily paste one onto one of the first few pages.

In order to determine the target date (recorded in the column to the right of the goal), estimate how many hours it would take to complete the task. In some cases, this is impossible to determine accurately. If so, simply guess, then add up to 50 percent to be on the safe side. For example, if you feel it could take 100 hours of solid writing to finish a project, make it 150 hours. Then divide this figure by the number of weeks you plan to work that year. For example, if you work 50 weeks, then the number of hours each week that you will have to work on your goal-related activity should be three. Since it is difficult to work steadily for three hours on any activity, break this into two sessions of one-and-a-half hours each. To accomplish your goal, you would have to spend one and-a-half hours twice per week in order to complete it by the end of the year. If this amount of time is unrealistic, set the goal for the end of the following year and work half as long each week. Don't be impatient; be realistic.

The continual recording of your major goals on each weekly page keeps your original intentions in mind. Each week you must now schedule an actual time in your weekly planner to work on that particular task. Treat these blocks of time as though they were appointments with important people (in fact they *are*, appointments with *yourself*.) By now you will already have appointments, meetings, etc., scheduled in your planner. You will have to work around these. But once your priority, goal-related activities have been scheduled, resist any temptation to use this time for less important "spur of the moment" things. Pretend they are appointments with your surgeon. Few people would delay life-saving surgery.

This method of actually determining the amount of time it will take to accomplish a goal forces you to be realistic. If you had ten goals, for instance, all requiring two hours each week to accomplish, it is unlikely you would be able to steal twenty hours each week to work on those special projects. You would have no time for your regular jobs (or for family time if you planned to work on the jobs in the evening.) But there's always next year. Boil those goals down to the few really meaningful accomplishments which would give you the greatest return on invested time. Be realistic. Leave spaces to accommodate the unexpected and to allow time for those items on the "to do" section. You should have a planner that breaks each day into time segments. Little blank squares for the days are not suitable for scheduling. Your planner is your most important time management tool, so choose it carefully. Of course, the only one that will work perfectly for you is one that you design for yourself. Don't overlook this possibility. Get into the habit of referring to it every morning. Follow it like a road map. Look at it again in the evening and make any necessary changes to the next day's plan.

Schedule your personal time as well

There's no way you're going to get more time than you have right now. But you can accomplish more and live more fully, if you budget the time that you do have. I have been talking primarily about scheduling work activities; but these may not be the first things you schedule into your planner.

Determine in advance how much time you want to

devote to the various activities in your life: work, family, recreation, rest, church, associations, education. Then schedule blocks of time on a planning calendar for these various activities. Start with family time and recreation, two activities that are usually neglected. Block out vacation time on the planner while the planner is still free from other encumbrances. Plan these vacations carefully. Consult your family and loved ones. Make commitments. Write confirming letters, reserve hotels and transportation. Then schedule professional development days, time you plan to spend with your family, and other special events. Consult the school calendar, your son's hockey schedule, the local baseball schedule, your city's activity calendar. If there's a long weekend you'd like to spend with the family away from home, block it off and make plans the following week.

Next, determine what education activities you want to participate in. Is there an evening course at the local college that would aid you professionally, personally, or spiritually? Any full-day seminars, weekend retreats, luncheon meetings? Block off the time on your planner, mark them, and then make the necessary arrangements to attend. Do you belong to any associations or would joining one aid in your development? If so, and there's still room in your planner to do it justice, mark it in there.

The order in which you block off the above activities is determined by the priority that you place on the various activities in your life. If you don't have a family, or if you feel education is more important, you would not plot them in the same sequence. Because there will be conflicts. You might not be able to attend school or church on a day you have set aside as a weekend of travel with the family, or vice versa. So it's important that you determine your priorities right at the start. This takes some soul searching. But once you've done it, don't compromise. Or you'll compromise your family and others right out of your life.

Remember that priorities are not always job-related. When pinpointing those important, meaningful activities, be sure to look at your total life.

Planning will help you say "no"

If you fail to plan, your time will be spent working on other people's priorities instead of your own. "Are you doing anything Friday night?" someone asks. "Not that I know of," you reply as you glance at your blank calendar. "Great! How about you and your mate dropping over to our place. We're showing the 16,000 slides we took of our trip to Europe." You grasp futilely for excuses but come up empty. You find yourself saying, "We'd love to." Afterwards you remember that you wanted to get that guest room painted on the weekend. Oh well, you can always do that later. After all, you've been delaying it since last winter anyway. What's another week or so?

People postpone activities that are important to them because of a reluctance to say *no*. And it's understandable; it's so easy to say *yes*. We avoid the immediate pain of disappointing someone, only to suffer a greater disappointment later because of an important job left unfinished.

When you plan, you determine what important tasks you would like to accomplish in the weeks and months ahead. Then you list the various steps (if more than one is required) in order to complete those tasks, and estimate the amount of time it would take to complete each step. To this you add a realistic safety factor to allow for interruptions, problems, etc., and schedule the total time in your planner.

Then, if someone asks if you're doing anything Friday night, a quick glance at your planner will prompt you to say, "Oh, I see we have a commitment that night. Why?" If anything has to be postponed, perhaps it should be that viewing of the 16,000 slides. It's easier to say *no* when a prior commitment has been made.

Many people waste time and accomplish little because of a lack of planning. Since TV networks plan their schedules well in advance, they know exactly what will be telecast Friday night. And if you don't have Friday night planned yourself, guess who loses by default?

Don't allow your calendar to fill up with other people's priorities while yours lie dormant on a wish list. Take charge of your own life by determining what you want to accomplish this month and this year. These are your goals. You will achieve them if you plan to achieve them. But planning is more than simply jotting these on a "to do" list; it is blocking off time in your planning calendar making an appointment with yourself. You are then obliged to keep that appointment, just as you are obliged to keep an appointment with your client, doctor, or close friend.

This doesn't mean you never say *yes* to a request, but it does mean you should evaluate the request to determine whether it is more important than the activity you are planning to work on during that time period. If it is more important, perhaps you should let it displace your planned activity. But never postpone your own plans simply because they *can* be postponed. Too often they are, again and again. Consequently, many plans are never realized and goals remain unachieved.

Say *no* or *yes* solely on the basis of the importance of the request compared to the importance of your own planned activity. And make sure you *do* plan; for those who don't plan are at the mercy of those who do.

Chapter 5

Time management with an electronic handheld computer

The Palm as a Personal Organizer

A good time management system should provide a simple way to highlight annual goals, schedule goal-related activities and other priorities into a planner and keep track of the myriad of other tasks that have to be done in the future. It should also facilitate note taking at meetings and during telephone conversations and provide instant access to data such as telephone numbers, statistics, documents, articles and client information. In addition, managers should be able to assign and keep track of projects, plan meetings and obtain feedback from staff and others. Ideally, the system should be portable, have the planner and various forms combined in one unit, be easy to access and have built-in reminders.

Until recently, such time-management systems have taken the form of multi-ring binders, some with a built-in planner, forms, note paper, pen and removable calculator. Generally called personal organizers and coming in various styles, shapes, and sizes, these systems had to be replenished weekly, monthly or quarterly. Data were entered manually, records handwritten, reminders visual, and articles and documents inserted manually into pockets or punched to fit the rings.

With technology, came electronic organizers in the form of handheld computers such as the Palm series. Initially these were used as accessories to the hard-copy organizers. Some manufacturers of the old-style organizers actually included compartments to hold the little computers while maintaining their own paper forms intact. It was as if to say, "Okay, if you want your electronic toy, we'll give you a place to put it; but don't expect it to replace the personal organizer." They didn't even bother to eliminate their telephone directory.

As time passed, and people experienced the ease with which they could access names and telephone numbers, events and things to do, they started using their Palms for other things as well. Eventually, most people realized it was more than an electronic directory/calendar/calculator/to do list combination. With the proper settings, some third-party software and a lot of experimentation, many people discovered that the tiny hand-held computer was a time management system itself. And that, in many respects, it was far superior to the hard-copy versions.

Small, slim and lightweight, the Palm has no rings to open or close, no forms to insert, sort, smear, smudge, remove or store. No dog-eared pages to flip or pens to replenish. And thankfully, no pockets in which to propagate piles of paper and coupons that expired in 1981. And the biggest advantage is not its size, but its memory, versatility, ease of operation and its ability to exchange data with a desktop or laptop computer.

In some of our time management workshops we show people how they can use their Palm handheld as a self-contained time management system that will help them manage their job, their time and their life. As a result, they increase their personal productivity and eliminate the frustration of not being able to access data instantly where and when they need it. They discover that they can complete projects and attend meetings on time, meet commitments as planned, maintain control of delegated assignments and keep their life in balance.

The Paper Planner versus the PDA

As Palms and other PDAs become more popular and

time management training becomes available for them, the debate as to whether handheld computers are better than hard copy planners continues to elevate. Although I prefer a paper planner for day to day scheduling, I used a Palm for a full year to evaluate it. Consequently most references in this chapter are to Palms as opposed to other handhelds on the market. There are still a few things that a Palm cannot do, like survive a drop from a three-story window or make its planner section large and legible while retaining its smallness. But then again, I have never seen a hard copy planner that could beam information to another planner or let you plan 30 years into the future or review schedules 90 years into the past. Here are a few pros and cons of both Palm hand-held computers and paper planners. Judge for yourself.

Two obvious advantages of the Palm are its portability and capacity. There are paper planners that are smaller and lighter, but their function is limited to little more than revealing the days of the year and room for a few scribbled appointments and events. It is impossible to purchase a hard copy planner that could hold even a fraction of the information provided by the Palm. If one were available, you would need a tractor-trailer to haul it around.

The paper planner still has its advantages. I have yet to see a Palm user write graffiti or peck at the miniature keyboard as quickly as a paper planner user could scribble appointments in their scheduler. When it comes to drawing maps and entering directions, they're way ahead. Even accessing data from the calendar at the flip of a page seems faster than turning on a Palm, tapping buttons and scrolling. You could even claim (poor handwriting aside) that a hard copy planner is a lot easier to read. And I have never known a paper planner user to have to change batteries or recharge it to keep it operating. The initial investment is a lot less for paper, as is the replacement cost if it's ever lost or damaged beyond repair. And speaking of costs, have you ever experienced a problem having to upgrade to the latest paper planner model? Paper planner users can also boast that they have never had their planner crash, freeze, or lose all their data. They might even mention the joy of being able to see their week at a glance, details and all, or being able to color code events without having to add third party software or simply the peace of mind they experience by seeing all their past year's planners lined up in their bookcase, information intact.

Lest you sense the argument swinging in favor of paper planners, let me remind you that dozens of past years' planners lined up in a row consume space and could escalate into clutter. I might even mention the destroyed trees that they represent. The total information contained in a life's accumulation of planners could be housed in a tiny 3 inch by 4½ inch Palm. There is unlimited space for notes and things to do. Only one entry for birthdays, anniversaries and other repeating events is necessary. No need to copy over information from one planner to the next. You don't even have to turn on your Palm to be reminded; an audible alarm will grab your attention. And when you mention readability, try reading a planner in the dark! I've yet to see a planner with a backlight.

Palms don't get smudged and dog-eared, nor worn or torn from too much erasing. They can make changes quickly and cleanly as well as keep confidential information hidden from sight. You can even attach notes to your appointments, scheduled tasks or to do items. You can beam assignments, business cards and other information to fellow Palm users, synchronize with your computer, and install e-books to utilize travel time.

Palms eliminate the need to carry a separate watch, calculator, alarm clock or expense forms. With third party software, you can include everything from time zones, area codes and metric conversion tables to flight schedules and medical information. Your Palm can serve as a digital camera, allow you to send and receive e-mail, and print your schedule directly from your Palm. Software is being developed daily that makes the Palm even more versatile.

The Palm may be more expensive initially, and be more fragile, but with a protective case and caution, it could serve you for the rest of your working days. It could even be cleared of its information and used by someone else. So the traditional planner, with its finite number of pages, space and time frame is being challenged with this relatively new electronic marvel. But is it really better? You be the judge. If it works for you, use it.

PDAs for planning are a personal preference

Personally, for the planning function at least, I prefer to use a hard copy planner where you can see your entire week, complete with scheduled tasks and descriptive things to do at a single glance.

It seems faster to retrieve information from a traditional planner, where a flip of a page brings you a whole new week of plans, appointments and projects. I abhor the thought of pecking at drop down menus with an oversized toothpick and writing, one letter at a time, on a slippery glass surface or punching individual letters on a miniature keyboard. I like the idea of seeing my activities take shape, being completed and remain visibly intact, as permanent trophies to my daily accomplishments. I like the look, feel and permanence of a hardcopy planner that also serves as a journal. And although I never thought of it before, perhaps I like the fact that a hard copy planner reflects an individual's uniqueness. It takes on the owner's personality, character, and thoughts. It reveals their habits and style. Every paper planner is different. It identifies the user and reveals something personal about him or her, while one Palm is like another - cold, impersonal and registered. And very expensive.

Like a growing number of other people who don't want to be left behind in this information age where technology is king, I continue to schedule in a hard copy planner while using my handheld computer for telephone directories and other databases. I like the idea of being able to HotSync with my desktop, and take relevant information with me when I travel. Some people also use their Palms for reading e-books, recording things to do, and reminding them of important events. Still others read and compose e-mail messages and jot down quick notes during telephone calls and meetings. Some use their handheld to record their goals, keep track of their assignments, or even beam their business card to others.

That's all very well. But when I witness people sending e-mail messages while they're driving and surfing the Internet at a family picnic, I cringe.

I have no interest in spending hours each day down-loading and testing shareware or using my Palm as a Global Positioning System, digital camera or T.V. channel changer. I simply want to make use of technology to increase my personal productivity. But I'm not averse to jotting down a quick note on a scratch pad or flipping pages in my planner or reading an article that's not electronic. I don't believe in using technology for technology's sake. I use it only when it's an obvious timesaver when the advantages overshadow any disadvantages.

Organizing your *To Do List*

If you use a Palm, you should use both your Date Book and your To Do List for items that you want to get done. The important, goal-related items are to be either scheduled at a specific time or listed at the top of the day's schedule as untimed events. The ones of lesser importance should be listed in their appropriated Category in your To Do List. It is important to develop a habit of reviewing both your Date Book and your To Do List every morning so that you are clear on your day's objectives and to make any necessary adjustments. Check them again at the end of your day, add any new tasks, check off completed ones and fine-tune your next day's schedule.

Prioritize the To Do items when you add them to your list and assign due dates. The Palm is set to sort the items in reducing order of priority, i.e. the default sorting order is Priority, Due Date. Change this to Due Date, Priority so that the jobs are listed by date due rather than by importance. This appears to fly in the face of good time management but you will that it works better. By assigning due dates to everything, you can easily avoid having too many things assigned to the same day. Each day's items will be grouped together so you will be able to spot them quickly. On any given day the highest priority ones are obvious by the assigned number, so you can work on those first. And remember, the really important items should not be on your To Do List anyway. They should be scheduled in your Date Book in specific time slots. The projects and tasks that are scheduled in your Date Book will yield 80 percent of your results.

Even if you show only uncompleted items, you could still have quite a long list of things to do. But don't be so quick to add Categories or have only the current days due items show. Out of sight, out of mind, and consequently you might forget to scroll through all your Categories. And if you don't choose to show all your uncompleted items, how will you ensure that you don't assign too many items to any particular day?

It's better to have a few long lists than many lists in different Categories. If all you're interested in are today's items, you won't have to scroll at all. And if you want to assign dates to new items or see what's listed for the days ahead, what's so hard about pushing the scroll button?

Having said all that, you might want to manage your tasks differently. The Palm allows many options and you should use the settings that work best for you. The important thing is to be realistic when deciding how many things to accomplish each day, avoid procrastination, and work on priorities first.

A great traveling companion

With the Palm you can travel light. In many cases you

won't even have to bring a laptop with you. Your Palm handheld computer can handle almost everything. When planning a business or pleasure trip, the first thing you should do is make up a travel checklist as a category in your To Do List. Jot down everything you have to do before you leave as well as everything you have to take with you. It might be wise to make several lists. With slight editing each time, they can become your perpetual checklists for all of your trips.

Prepare a business card specifically for beaming to other Palm users that you meet. Attach a memo that highlights your products or services so that your business card becomes a promotion tool as well. If you plan to meet with several people during the trip, include directions to their offices or homes as attachments to their names in your Date Book.

When you book flights, make hotel reservations and confirm appointments, enter the data into your Palm immediately. Enter your flight departure time in Date Book as an appointment and attach a note bearing all the information such as flight number, seat selection, airport terminal, and frequent flyer numbers. Then enter your arrival time with a note indicating hotel name, address, phone number and confirmation number.

Before heading off on the trip, Hot Sync your palm so it's up to date and bring a recharger kit or spare batteries with you. Download an e-book or two for reading during the flight or before retiring in your hotel room. Reset the time on your Palm to coincide with your destination so any alarms will sound at the right time. And don't forget to create an Ideas category in your Memo Pad so you can jot down all those creative ideas that occur to you en route.

If you plan to do a lot of typing while you're away, invest in a collapsible keyboard. It's great for taking notes at meetings, typing reports or finishing off that best-selling novel. Bring a spare stylus with you just in case.

Be sure to enter expenses into your Palm as they occur, as well as new contact names and other information. Don't procrastinate or you'll cause a time problem for yourself later. As soon as you return from the trip, perform a HotSync so you'll have all the information on your desktop

Traveling with a Palm - a case study

Several years ago my laptop was giving me problems. During a trip to Austin, Texas it crashed completely leaving me stranded. Palm to the rescue. With the portable Palm keyboard I was able to continue writing with some semblance of efficiency. And the modem that I had purchased for my Vx Palm allowed me to access, send and receive e-mail from my hotel room. Now, of course, there are devices such as the BlackBerry that are completely wireless and allow you to send and receive e-mail at will. My sudden reliance on the dinky hand-held computer highlighted its usefulness. I had never been able to slip my laptop into my jacket pocket as I could my Palm. Nor had I ever used it for a wake-up call or as a timing device during presentations. In the latter case I used Big Clock, freeware that I had downloaded from www.palmgear.com. The digital clock face filled the screen, and could even be seen by someone near-sighted like me.

I found myself calculating the tip in the back of a taxi, adding the total sales at my trade show booth and quickly retrieving data such as our UPS account number, hotel confirmation number and travel itinerary. I was even able to beam some presentation notes to my portable BJC 50 printer without any problem. I had brought printer cables with me to use with my Sony laptop since I hadn't been able to get the beaming option to work. The chap at the store where I purchased it told me it was very difficult to do. It sure worked well with the Palm!

Other than having to borrow a laptop for my PowerPoint presentation (which I had dumped onto a CD in the event of such an emergency) it was a rather pleasant experience. A fellow speaker recently shared that with her Treo 650 phone with Cingular Wireless coverage she can run PowerPoint presentations from the phone. Presenter-To-Go from Margi (http://www.margi.com) is needed to get the presentation onto the phone and then onto the LCD projector, but it simplifies things even more. Technology continues to change.

Before you leave on a trip, make sure you change the clock if you're traveling to a different time zone. I didn't, and found myself being awakened at 4 am. Unless you're a very light sleeper, set the alarm at the loudest setting. To do this, go to Preferences select General (top right hand corner, to bring up the proper screen. This is where you change the time as well.) Use the drop down menu opposite Alarm Sound to select High. When setting your alarm go to Date Book, tap the hour that you want to get up and on the Set Time screen that appears, select the exact time you want to be awakened. Then with that time highlighted in Date Book, tap Details.

On the Event Details screen, make sure Alarm is checked. Just to the right of this box you might want to change the advance warning to 1 minute. (You don't want to get up too early!) Check OK to return to the Date Book screen and tap the date at the top left of the screen, select Options and then Preferences. On the Preferences screen that appears, select the Alarm Sound that is most likely to jar you awake. I prefer Wake Up but someone else suggested Concerto. Take your pick. Then set the Remind Me option at 10 times, just in case. Finally, on the same screen, select Play Every Minute. With the Palm device out of its case and on the bedside table just a few feet from your ear, you should rest easy that you wouldn't sleep through that wake-up call. Just make sure you don't use those settings when you're in a meeting!

Retrieving information from your Palm

The biggest problem with filing systems is that most people have trouble finding material weeks or even days after they file it. This is just as true for electronic files as it is for paper files. Sometimes, they don't even know what they're looking for! For example, have you ever experienced the need to find some information that you knew was contained in some memo or letter or report - but couldn't remember which memo, letter or report it was in? Well, you could have the same problem with the Palm. It has an excellent Find function; but you have to know what to look for. So use attached Notes if necessary whenever you create names and addresses, memos or documents. Ask yourself what you would think of if you were looking for this item in the future. If you feel you might think of memory systems or forgetfulness or mind training, then jot those words onto an attached note. Searching for any of those words will take you to the Note, which, in turn, will lead you to the Memo itself.

This is particularly useful with your Address Book. Many people have trouble remembering the name of someone they had only met briefly at a meeting, conference or dinner party. Yet they have no trouble remembering the event itself. So jot down words such as, Met at office show, or NAPO Conference, or Friend of John Smith. Searching for any of those words will immediately take you to the note and then the name (which of course you will recognize the moment you see it.) When creating documents or making Address Book entries, always think ahead as to what you might need the information for in the future. Build an identifying key word into the data. Is the person a prospect, fellow association member, or Palm user? Build the relevant key word into the entry and you can immediately find all your prospects, club members or networking associates using the Find function. This could be either included in one of the fields or as an attached note. When you start a search, do so in the Application where it is most likely located. The search always begins in the current Application and it may save you a little time.

Just like a filing cabinet or a computer, the more stuff you have filed, the harder it is to locate anything. So delete and purge on a regular basis. Don't keep completed items if the only advantage is to boast about all your accomplishments. Get rid of all information that is of no further use. And remember, you will never waste time searching for something if you know you don't have it.

The alarming side of the Palm

One of the most basic, yet most effective, time management techniques is to write things down. There's no way we can remember or keep track of the dozens of projects, tasks, assignments and activities going on at any one time. And most people have little trouble following that principle, albeit some are more structured and organized than others in doing so. They make lists of things to do, schedule their major tasks and all of their appointments, jot down reminders to make telephone calls, record follow-up dates on assignments, indicate when they have to make purchases and write down a myriad of other chores, tasks and personal commitments.

The trouble is, most people still don't get everything done on time and frequently miss items altogether. In spite of writing things down, they still forget. Either they're so engrossed in a task that they forget a previously planned appointment or they don't get an opportunity to review their To Do List. That's why alarms are so important. They don't let you forget. They remind you of the right thing at the right time. No matter how immersed in an activity you happen to be at a given time, they draw your attention to the priority of the moment. So if you want to make an important call at a specific time during the day, don't simply enter the obligation in your Date Book. Add an alarm as well. This applies to any call that you are expecting at a specific time as well. Set the alarm to chime a few minutes in advance so you will have an opportunity to prepare. If you have to attend a meeting, set the alarm far enough in advance so you will have time to get there. You want to be reminded when it's time to leave the office, not when it's time to be at the meeting.

Don't be an alarmaholic. You don't need alarms to chime for every task you schedule. If you have formed the habit of walking every morning or visiting the Y every lunch hour or watering the plants before bedtime every night, you certainly don't need alarms to remind you. But for important tasks, meetings or appointments, alarms are the way to go.

To set an alarm, select the time of the activity, tap Details, and place a checkmark in the Alarm box. Don't have the alarm set at a level that wakes the neighbors - unless you're hard of hearing. Tap on the Preferences icon and set the Alarm Sound at Low. This will affect all your alarms so don't forget to change it when you use your Palm as an alarm clock or you store it in a desk drawer while you are working. If you are continually checking your Palm, you may not need an audible sound at all; the large reminder note that fills the screen may be sufficient. In this case, set the alarm at the Off position.

It's annoying to others when an alarm goes off in movie theatre, restaurant, church or other public place. This includes workplace meetings and cafeterias. Be sensitive to other people. If everyone left their Palm alarms, beepers and cellular phones turned on all the time, libraries would be noisier than Radio City Music Hall.

Alarms are useful. Used wisely, they will improve your personal productivity and promptness. Used with discretion, they will improve your interpersonal relationships as well.

PDAs require manual labor

Who has time to read the manual? It's almost as thick as the Dummies book, with smaller print! Anyway, the Palm is a breeze to operate. At least, that's what we think. Press the Telephone hard button (Address Book) and names and addresses pop into view. Tap on New and a self-explanatory template appears. This is a piece of cake. We find we can enter names and addresses, enter appointments in Date Book, even write a Memo by picking at the miniature keyboard with a stylus (because we find it's too easy to make errors using Graffiti.)

We find the Palm is really a fun thing to use. It makes a fantastic Address Book. And we always know what day it is. In fact, most of us have learned how to set alarms, enter untimed events and keep a long list of things to do. We feel we must be taking advantage of almost every feature the Palm has to offer. It hasn't allowed us to throw away our hard copy planner, or eliminate our Personal Organizer, or our telephone Log or Delegation Record or Meeting forms or .... Wait a minute! Are we sure that we are using the Palm as it could - and should - be used?

The average person uses less than ten percent of the Palm's capability. Most people don't know the quick commands, such as /L that makes the Address Book appear. They haven't entered shortcuts that would allow them to insert a phrase or sentence by writing only two letters. Many people are not familiar with beaming business cars, attaching notes, marking data as private or increasing Graffiti speed and accuracy.

The problem is manual labor. They haven't labored with the manual long enough. It's not surprising. Most people don't even read the manual for the $40,000 car they bought, so why should they bother with the manual for a $400 handheld device? But the time invested reading the manual will not only yield far greater time savings in more efficient operation of the Palm, it will allow a much greater and more effective utilization of the Palm as well.

Further reading, or participation in training workshops will yield even greater results. Learn to use third party software and techniques that will convert your Palm - or whatever electronic device you are using - into a complete time management system. Make notes and ensure follow-up at meetings and during telephone conversations. Keep track of your assignments on a delegation record. Use your Date Book as a planning system and track the progress of your goals. Integrate your To Do list with your Date Book. Get more done in less time with less stress by investing time in learning the true potential of your Palm. A little manual labor goes a long way.

Chapter 6

Organize your office and yourself

Engineer an office environment that saves time

Ever visit Caesar's Palace in Las Vegas? The environment there actually *encourages* you to spend time and money. Moving sidewalks take you inside (but leaving isn't as convenient).You must pass the gambling casino in order to get to the registration desk. After registering you have to wind your way through the gaming tables to get to the elevators. You're tempted. And when you start to gamble, it's so easy to continue. The drinks are free. The chairs are comfortable. Air conditioning and loud colors keep you from getting drowsy. There are no clocks on the walls. No windows. You lose track of time. The dealers pay off in larger denomination chips. You lose more and faster. The chips are only negotiable at Caesar's so you don't readily move to another casino. It's easy to buy chips at any table; but you have to find the casino cashier if you want to cash them in. Everything is conducive to the spending of time and money.

Take a lesson from Caesar's Palace. Develop an office environment that encourages the *saving* of time and money. If you can influence the layout of the main office do so. Arrange the desks to coincide with the work flow. Place office equipment so as to minimize steps, while keeping in mind the possible distractions. Decentralize storage cabinets so everyone's supplies are close at hand. If you need a centralized storage room, make sure it's easy to locate the various supplies. Try painting the shelves in the supply cupboard different colors. All stationery, letterhead, forms and paper products could be kept on the green shelf, all computer and other office equipment supplies on the red shelf, all small office supplies such as paper clips, rubber bands, staples, etc., on the blue shelf, and so on. Everyone would soon get to know that they could find the printer cartridges on the red shelf and the sticky notes on the blue shelf, and it would make it easier to tell new employees and visitors where to find something.

Don't skimp on inexpensive equipment. Everyone should have their own stapler, 3-hole punch, pencil sharpener or whatever items they use frequently. Don't run out of supplies or stationery. Organize the storage so there's a place for everything. Insist on everything being kept that way. For forms, letterhead, envelopes, promotion material, tape a copy to the outside of the box for easy identification. Number the cartons 1, 2, 3, etc., when they come in. Stack them in reverse order and when you get down to 2, re-order.

Have written procedures for all tasks. Have the employees who are responsible for the tasks make up the procedures. Review them. Refine them. Simplify them if possible. And make everyone in the office aware of them. If necessary, get a large wall calendar. Record all meetings, conferences, business trips, vacations, important deadlines so they're visible to everyone. Investigate any high-tech office equipment or gadgets that may save you time.

Organize your private office

A survey conducted by Steelcase Canada some time ago revealed that 74 percent of office workers feel they could do more work in the same amount of time if office conditions were changed. The three factors office workers said could help them increase their productivity are improved work flow between people and departments, reduction of noise and distraction in the office, and access to proper job equipment.

Make sure your private office is arranged so as to attract a minimum of interruptions. Don't face the open doorway. Have your desk to one side, so people will have to go out of their way to see you. Or have your desk facing away from the doorway. If they are able to catch your eye from outside the office they will be tempted to walk inside and strike up a conversation. For the same reason, avoid having gathering spots outside your office such as coffee or photocopying facilities. One manager reported that the coffee maker was right outside his office door and people would kill time while the coffee brewed by walking into his office and socializing.

Although the absence of chairs would make unscheduled visitations brief, it would also make scheduled meetings inconvenient. But don't have chairs close to your desk or facing you unless you're short of space. They're an open invitation for people to slip into them. Instead, place them about six feet or more from the desk, and have them facing each other. The awkwardness of sitting that far away or the inconvenience of dragging one to your desk should discourage anyone from heading for the chairs. When the drop-in approaches your desk, you can stand, and remain standing until the brief conversation is over. If you want to carry on a lengthy conversation, simply move from your desk to the chairs and carry on the conversation in the open, facing each other, without the barrier of a desk between you.

Have your office decorated tastefully, but simply. A

lot of family photos, trophies, certificates, and citations will encourage chit chat. Don't have ashtrays if you don't smoke. Or comfortable sofas if you don't sleep in your office. But plants are great, even if you don't garden. And a clock is a great reminder of the speed at which time passes. Place it where your visitor can see it.

Arrange your working tools and furniture closely around your desk area. Don't place frequently used filing cabinets or bookcases on the other side of the room. You should have everything at your fingertips. Have an adequate inventory of felt pens, paper clips, staples, highlighter markers, etc., in one of your desk drawers. Sharing with other people is not economical when you take lost time into consideration.

Your desk does not have to be large but you must have sufficient working area. The desk is not meant for storage, so keep it clear of paperwork except for projects you are working on. Other projects should be retained in a follow-up file; the bulkier ones can be kept in colored manila folders, clearly identified. These should be kept in hanging files in your desk drawer. If your desk doesn't have a drawer large enough to hold files, I recommend you get one that does. If this is impossible, keep the follow-up file system and project files in a vertical step file. Keep them on the top of your desk in a plastic rack or in a filing cabinet to the side of your desk.

The use of binders

Keep in 3-ring binders those articles, procedures, job descriptions, policies, product bulletins and anything else that you refer to frequently. Binders are great for storing articles, newspaper clippings, reports and other information that you want to keep for reference. Here are a few tips for using them:

♦   Make sure they are large enough for the amount of material you hope to accumulate on a specific topic. Half inch or one inch binders are useless for categories such as "computer technology" or "time management". You would have to make up about ten binders within a few years.

♦   Don't divide the categories too finely or you'll be overrun with binders containing only a few sheets each. "Time Management" may be sufficient. When your binder is full, break out the largest subcategory such as "Meetings". When the original binder becomes full again, break out the next largest category, and so on. Your binders will increase in number only as the amount of research material increases.

♦   To file newspaper clippings, paste the article on 8 1/2 x 11, 3-ring paper. Don't keep a separate file folder filled with newspaper clippings.

♦   For larger newspaper articles, you may want to 3-hole punch the item itself. But I recommend you pho-tocopy it first and keep the photocopy. A copy is stronger, and will not fade and become discolored.

♦ When clipping or tearing out articles, be sure to note the source and date on the margin of the article. You may need this when using the information later, either to give credit, seek permission to reprint, or simply to obtain more information. Example, *Writer's Digest, July/06, pg. 60-61.*

♦ Identify the binders so they can be identified quickly. Use different colored insert cards, or better still a cartoon of the picture representing the category. Example: a clock for "time management", a picture of a computer for "computers", etc. You will be able to identify the binder at a glance. The bookcase or shelf should be within reach. Surround yourself on three sides with your working materials.

♦ If you're into technology, remember that most of these notes, article segments etc. can be scanned into computer files, with a huge increase in time savings and ease of use.

Control your environment

Your office should be arranged so that everything is readily accessible. Every time you have to walk to the main office for supplies, you risk an extended interruption. So anticipate the envelopes, letterhead, pads, etc., that you will need, and include them in your inventory. If you need an extra cabinet or shelf on the wall near your desk, get one. Don't let your office environment control you. You spend too many hours there to suffer unnecessary inconveniences. If a fixture prevents you from placing your desk where you want it, have the fixture removed. If the door is in the wrong place, change it. If the lighting is poor, add more lights. If the rollers on your chair are worn, replace them. Any costs incurred are one-time costs; the time savings are forever. Experiment with several arrangements until you get the one that works best for you.

Couches are too comfortable and encourage socializing, but chairs placed around a conference table encourage results. Move the telephone so you have your back to the door when using it. This removes the temptation to be distracted by anyone walking into your office. You can't pay attention to two people at the same time.

If you don't have an office, do what you can to build privacy into your "territory". Use dividers, bookcases, plants, and filing cabinets to shield yourself from eye contact with other people. Locate your desk away from the main thoroughfare of traffic if possible. Researchers have concluded that privacy encourages job satisfaction and increases performance. Try to surround yourself with some protection, even if it's only a free-standing divider or two. Aim for good ones. Make sure they're tall enough to prevent people from peering over, and sound proof enough to prevent them from talking through. Try for an inch or more of sound absorbing material on both sides, and a solid center. Don't leave yourself vulnerable to interruption from everyone who passes your desk.

If you are unable to hide your desk, at least hide your eyes so everyone doesn't feel compelled to talk to you. A strategically placed plant, filing cabinet, or stand-up portrait ought to do the trick. If your eyes meet those of every passerby, you are asking to be interrupted.

Personalize your filing system

File your material so it's easy to retrieve. If you feel you will never need to retrieve it, scrap it. Use hanging folders appropriately labeled. Store them in similarly labeled manila folders so you will always return the folder to the right spot. (Your hanging folders need never leave the drawer or cabinet). You could file alphabetically according to category, e.g.: Suppliers, A to Z; Administration, A to Z; Buildings and Equipment, A to Z, etc.

Articles, job descriptions, board meeting minutes, newsletters, bulletins, and anything else you refer to frequently could be kept in 3-ring binders. Label them clearly for easy identification. Purge your files regularly; resist the urge to buy more filing cabinets.

Brief clippings from newspapers and magazines, one-liners, ideas, could be pasted onto 3 x 5 index cards and filed according to category. But don't do anything manually if a computer will do it for you faster.

If you read something that you will want to use later, it's generally a good idea to photocopy that page, or type the idea on a card and file it under the appropriate category. Alternatively, you could jot down the book and page number on an index card and file that in the appropriate spot.

The alpha-numerical file

A simple filing system that eliminates misfiling, makes retrieval easy, and assures that something retrieved from the files is put back in the same spot again, is the alpha-numerical system. Here, each category has a reference file folder containing a listing of all sub-headings within that category. Each sub-heading is assigned a number, and that number only, not the heading, is marked on the file folders within that category.

For example, assume you have a category title

"Publishing". Take a folder, mark the tab with the word "Publishing", and inside that folder tape an 8 1/2 x 11 sheet of lined paper, and head it up "Publishing". Under this heading, list all the sub-categories or sub-headings that you need. Don't bother to list them alphabetically. It's easy to glance down the list later to find the sub-heading you are looking for, as long as the list doesn't go beyond one page in length.

Now assign a number series to this "Publishing" category. If it's "100", mark "100" opposite the word "Publishing" on the index tab of the main reference file folder. Then opposite the sub-headings, assign numbers 101, 102, 103, etc. Next, mark these numbers on a set of file folders, and file the papers in these folders, marking the same number on each piece of paper you file.

For example, if one of your sub-headings is "book clubs" and it had been assigned the number "106", you would mark "106" on the piece of paper to be filed there. When you want to retrieve it from the file later, turn to the reference file folder, glance down the list until you see "book clubs", note the number opposite it, and pull out the appropriate folder. To re-file, simply stick it in the folder bearing the same number that appears on the piece of paper. Misfiling is unlikely, even when dozens of people are using the same files.

With this system it is easy to add, eliminate, or combine categories. Since no titles appear on the individual folders, it is easy to use the numbered folders for other sub-categories if the existing sub-category is eliminated.

The more time spent in filing a piece of correspondence, the less time spent in retrieval. But how often do you have to retrieve something from the files? It may be more economical and faster to set up a simple system based on topic or date. One administrative assistant insists that filing by date is faster, even for retrieval. She claims her boss is always asking for a letter that he received "about a month ago" or "last January or February". So she has labeled the folders by the month, regardless of the topic or person originating the letter. Set up a system that satisfies your needs. And remember, the name of the game is retrieval, not storage.

If it's your assistant that does the actual filing, make it as easy as possible for him or her. If it's your memo, letter or report, you probably know where it should be filed. So jot down this information at the top of the paper. Also, the throw-out date, if you don't plan to keep if forever. If it has to be followed up later, note the follow-up date so your assistant can stick it in the follow-up file under the appropriate date. It's easier to jot a few words on each piece of paper than to have your assistant guess at what to do with it.

Electronic-assisted filing

If you want to eliminate the bulk of the paperwork in your office, you might consider document imaging, where paper is scanned, indexed and stored on optical disks or CD ROMs. On the other hand, if you don't want to destroy the paperwork, but want to be able to access it easily, you could investigate a paper management program available from The Monticello Corporation. Check their website at www.thepaper-tiger.com for details on this paper management program. To file a document you enter any number of key words you might associate with it, along with the physical location of the file, into *The Paper Tiger* database. The files can be either alphabetical or numerical. Numerical is preferred for the same reasons mentioned for the manual alpha-numerical file system described earlier.

Hints for effective filing

Here is a checklist of things to keep in mind when working with filing systems.

♦ Label all your files clearly.

♦ Keep a record of your file headings.

♦ Keep your file categories as small as possible.

♦ Never have a miscellaneous file.

♦ Purge your files at least once a year.

♦ Store old files; don't file them!

♦ Mark key papers with a colored marker or label.

♦ Keep often-used files together

♦ Keep key documents, certificates, etc., together.

♦ Keep your files thin, no more than 1/2 inch thick.

♦ Have frequently used files close at hand, e.g., in

your desk drawer, credenza or in a mobile filing unit.

◆When filing, use colored tabs for alphabetical groupings or categories.

◆File daily, don't let paperwork pile up.

◆Staple reply letters to originals. Don't use paper clips.

◆ Arrange correspondence according to the day of writing, with the most recent communication at the front.

◆ Chart information required on an on-going basis, such as sales figures, returns and allowances, production figures. Don't spend time each month digging through past records.

◆ Use hanging files. Don't jam manila folders into a drawer or filing cabinet by themselves. Manila folders used in conjunction with hanging files are ideal for easy retrieval.

◆ Beware of double filing. Don't duplicate files.

◆ Allow three to four inches of work-space in a drawer. Avoid tugging and damaging folders.

◆ Have a different colored tab for each year. Keep current years more accessible. Thin out or throw out past years.

If you have trouble organizing your desk, files, office or home, there are professional organizers who will not only help you in the initial cleanup stage, but will recommend the equipment, supplies and furniture, as well as provide the training, encouragement and support needed to stay organized. Contact the *National Association For Professional Organizers* at www.napo.net. With over three thousand members, there's a good chance one will be located in your area. In Canada, contact *Professional Organizers in Canada* at www.organizersincanada.com.

Chapter 7

Add structure to your life

Develop a personal organizer

Do you have the cost on those digital recorders yet?" the voice on the line asks impatiently.

"Oh yes, Sam," you reply, digging through a pile of messages. "Bill gave me the figures over the phone earlier today." You start shuffling through the paper on your desk. "Now where's that scrap of paper," you grumble to yourself. "It was here a minute ago." There's an awkward pause, some time-killing small talk, then an embarrassing delay as you can't seem to locate the figures.

"Well look, just give me Bill's number, and I'll check it myself," the frustrated voice snaps in your ear. "Maybe that's just as well," you agree. "He was discussing some options that you might want to consider...."

You rush to rationalize the inconvenience that you have caused, while trying to recall where you put Bill's number. Then you *do* recall. You never recorded it. Bill had initiated the call, you were busy at the time, and it just hadn't occurred to you to ask for it. "I'm afraid I don't seem to have his number anywhere," you eventually tell him. Sam makes some remark to the effect that he'll get the number somewhere else, and mercifully hangs up. "Oh boy," you sigh to yourself, "If I could only develop a system that automatically records all calls and telephone numbers, notes all phone numbers, summarizes the significant points from any conversation and highlights all the follow-ups required."

You *can* develop such a system. And regardless of how conscientiously you apply time management strategies discussed in books and articles, unless you *do* develop effective systems, you won't be able to avoid situations like the one described above.

Time is lost, money wasted, problems created, and tempers primed, all because of a reluctance or neglect on the part of people to write things down. Most people overestimate their memories and underestimate their busyness. And they discover, too late, that their intentions had been lost in the heat of the battle.

After all, how could we remember to carry out that directive when we had to immediately reach for a ringing telephone? And no wonder we forgot to follow up on that telephone request with two people simultaneously bursting into our office! We hop from one task to another, dozens of thoughts spinning in our minds. When a new thought occurs we frequently interrupt what we're working on to pursue it before it escapes us. We're constantly juggling tasks and interrupting our staff. Occasionally we jot things down; but on scraps of paper, the backs of envelopes, or "to do" lists which get lost in the shuffle.

To be effective we must be organized. This involves creating a system of recording that will eliminate the need to interrupt our employees or the task at hand and prevent us from forgetting those messages, directives, and ideas that rain upon us. If you are adept at using electronic handheld computers such as the Palm, you could adapt the following ideas to your PDA as explained briefly in Chapter 5. Otherwise, make up the following forms for a binder or purchase one ready made at www.taylorintime.com.

Telephone & Visitor's Log

There are two major categories of follow-ups that tend

to fall through the cracks; those received via the telephone or personal visits and those that we think of ourselves, those ideas that pop into our heads when we least expect them. For the first category, draw up a *Telephone and Visitor's Log* form. Keep it simple, with space for the name, company, and telephone number of the caller. Divide the sheet into two vertical columns labeled *Nature of Business* and *Action Required*. Every time you answer the phone or receive a visitor, quickly jot the information into this log, summarizing the key points on the left side and using the right side only when action is required as a result of the call. Even if the phone rings incessantly or a steady stream of visitors invades your office, you won't forget to follow up on anything. It's all there in writing. When you have completed the task, cross out the notation on the right side of the log. A quick scan of the pages will tell you whether there's anything left undone.

Try it. Keep a binder containing these forms on your desk. Have it opened at the day's date ready for action. When you make or receive a call, automatically pull the binder in front of you and, instead of doodling on a scrap of paper as you talk, make notes in the *Nature of Business* area. You will be recording information that you may need in the future, even though you may not realize it at the time. When the person at the other end of the line makes a request, jot it down in the *Action Required* area. Record the name and company of the caller at the start or during a pause in the conversation. Before you hang up, be sure to get the phone number, even if you already have it in your directory. It only takes a second for the person to give it; it could take ten times that long for you to look it up.

Exhibit 4

Telephone & Visitor's Log

NAME _____   DATE _____

COMPANY _____   TIME _____

NUMBER _____

NATURE OF BUSINESS

CALL	☐
VISIT	☐
INITIATED BY:	
MYSELF	☐
OTHER PARTY	☐
TIME: _____	

ACTION REQUIRED

LENGTH
OF
CALL
MINUTES

NAME _____   DATE _____

COMPANY _____   TIME _____

NUMBER _____

NATURE OF BUSINESS

CALL	☐
VISIT	☐
INITIATED BY:	
MYSELF	☐
OTHER PARTY	☐
TIME: _____	

ACTION REQUIRED

LENGTH
OF
CALL
MINUTES

Form No. P1

Now you have a great back-up system. You can relate who called, when, about what, and the nature of the action requested, even months later. Can your memory do that? If requests or even the phone calls have ever slipped your mind this is not just a time saver, it is a must.

The form shown in Exhibit 4 has space to indicate whether the telephone call was initiated by yourself or the other party, the length of the call, and the time the call was made or received. This additional information allows you to determine the time of the day when most calls are received so you can schedule your quiet hours, lunch hours, breaks, etc. accordingly. It also flags the "long-winded" callers, or tells you that you are spending excessive time talking to certain individuals. You may find, as many people do, that 80 percent of your telephone time is spent talking to 20 percent of your callers.

This *Telephone and Visitor's Log* can protect your back as well. People tend to have short memories. They feel they have been waiting "weeks" for materials they had requested only a few days earlier. A typical experience might be "Harold, I just received fifty folders in the mail. I asked for 100, and that was about two weeks ago!"

"Oh, I thought you had only asked for fifty. And it didn't seem that long ago," I reply.

"No, it was 100", he might insist, "and it was at least two weeks ago when I called you. And quite frankly I'm annoyed with the lack of service I'm getting from you people."

"I'm sorry, you're probably right. I have a terrible memory. Just a second, I'll check it out..." While talk-

Exhibit 5

Perpetual
Telephone & Visitor's Log

COMPANY _____	CONTACT_____
ADDRESS_____	INFO.
_____	
TELEPHONE _____	

DATE	TIME	ITEMS DISCUSSED	ELAPSED TIME	ACTION REQUIRED
			TIME: _____	
			LENGTH OF CALL MINUTES	
			TIME: _____	
			LENGTH OF CALL MINUTES	
			TIME: _____	
			LENGTH OF CALL MINUTES	
			TIME: _____	
			LENGTH OF CALL MINUTES	

Form No. P6

ing, I would flip the pages until I came to his call.

"Oh, here it is. No, the call was made last Tuesday, Sam. And you did ask for 100 originally. But it's crossed out. Something about not including the committee members in this distribution…"

"Oh, that's right, I forgot about that. And it was only last week?!"

"Yes, Tuesday, 10:15 a.m.."

A pause, "What do you do, record all your calls?" he might ask.

"Yes, I do. I want to make sure that nothing falls through the cracks. We hate to let people down."

Those may not be the exact words, but let it be known that you make notes. It's for their benefit primarily. But it also discourages them from exaggerating or distorting the truth a little. And it's amazing how they tend *not* to exaggerate in the future!

It's embarrassing (and sometimes costly) to forget what you quoted a client during a previous conversation. Or that you even *had* a previous conversation! Some people, who now use a telephone log, claim they used to forget the name of the person before they even finished the conversation! Now, since the name is the first thing recorded, they are never embarrassed by not being able to recall the person's name at the end of the conversation

Although the *Telephone & Visitor's Log* prevents embarrassment and "protects your back", it is primarily intended to eliminate some of those time wasters caused by forgetfulness or lack of concentration or failure to listen. It's difficult not to listen when you are actually making notes on what is being said. And there's less likelihood that you'll be distracted by visitors walking

103

Exhibit 6

Alternative Telephone & Visitor's Log

DATE _____

Date/Time:	Notes:	Action Required:
_____		
Name/Company:		
_____		
_____		
_____		
_____		
Telephone No.:		Date Completed:
_____		_____

Date/Time:	Notes:	Action Required:
_____		
Name/Company:		
_____		
_____		
_____		
_____		
Telephone No.:		Date Completed:
_____		_____

Date/Time:	Notes:	Action Required:
_____		
Name/Company:		
_____		
_____		
_____		
_____		
Telephone No.:		Date Completed:
_____		_____

Form No. P1A

into your office. There's an almost irresistible urge to try to carry on two conversations at once, one conversation consisting mainly of hand motions to a drop-in visitor. If someone walks into your office uninvited while you're on the phone, ignore that person. The caller was there first. Just keep making notes until the call is finished.

Use this *Telephone & Visitor's Log* for both incoming and outgoing calls. In the latter case you can jot down the items you wish to discuss in that left-hand section and check them off as you discuss them. This way, nothing will be forgotten and you won't have to make a second call. If the person is not in when you call and you leave a message to call you back at a specific time, write "to call back between 3 and 4" in that *Action Required* section. This will act as a flag in the event that the person doesn't call back as requested. Some people don't return calls promptly, if at all. Especially if it's information that *you* want. You may want to call again if you need the information before a certain date. How many times have you left a message, never received a call-back, and forgot to follow up? When you call again and reach your party, simply cross off that "to call back" notation and away you go.

The same form can be used when someone drops into your office (by invitation hopefully.) Making a note of the request can only impress the visitor with your obvious intention to take action afterwards.

This all sounds very easy. But be careful. You may find you "forget" to use the log. Or it gets put away somewhere. Or it's not opened and you can't be bothered going through the hassle of recording what will probably be a brief call. It takes persistence. Force yourself to use it for a week. The second week it will become easier. Soon after that it will become a habit. And remember, habits are hard to break, even the good ones!

The form you use is not important; the important thing is that you use it. I have developed three different types of *Telephone & Visitor's Log* forms as shown in the Exhibits. One is a *perpetual* one that records all the calls to the same person on the one form. These are great for clients, and are filed behind alphabetical tabs. You could even use a simple steno pad. Draw a vertical line two-thirds of the way across the page, do your note-taking on the left side of the line, and record any actions required as a result of the call on the right side of the line. Or you could purchase forms, *Telephone Log Booklets* or a portable *Personal Organizer* that contains a section of these *Telephone and Visitor's Log* forms from Harold Taylor Time Consultants Inc. Other companies may have similar products that will do just as good a job.

The objective of using this form should be to take action, not just to have a record of the call. Don't allow those follow-ups to sit on your form for long. Do them, schedule a time to do them in your planner, assign them to someone else, or add them to that list of things to accomplish tomorrow. Throw out most of the forms once you have extracted any needed information, such as telephone numbers, addresses, etc. Some of the forms containing key information could be filed chronologically for future reference. But don't allow them to build up indefinitely.

Delegation Record

In addition to telephone calls, you should also make a

note of any ideas that pop into your mind while you are working, traveling, or at play. This would prevent the following scenario. You're busy writing a letter at the office when you suddenly think of a report that you want your assistant to prepare. Not wanting to forget the assignment, you interrupt your train of thought and call your assistant. "Sorry to bother you," you begin, "but I just thought of something…" and you go on to explain the assignment in detail. After you hang up it takes several minutes to review what you were working on and get re-oriented to the task. As if interrupting yourself wasn't bad enough, you have just wasted your assistant's time as well.

If this happens to you, did you even stop to think what your assistant might have been doing when your interruption came? Typing a letter? Talking to a client? In the middle of a telephone call? Whatever it was, it now takes longer to complete and you have succeeded in being somebody else's time waster.

If you only interrupt your employees a few times each day, that's not bad. But most managers interrupt them continually. As soon as they think of something, they grab for the telephone (or worse still, interrupt in person) before the thought escapes them. "Oh, Jack, before I forget…" or "Sorry to bother you again, Jan, but I just thought of something else…".

Forgetting about the effect on the employees, can you imagine the minutes lost by the manager if there are five employees being interrupted four times each in the course of the day? And how many of those interruptions couldn't be delayed for a half day or more without any detrimental effect on your organizational goals? The answer will probably be "none" or "very few". We tend to act impulsively, "before we forget". Unfortunately, in doing so we are impeding our employees' productivity as well as our own.

To take care of those ideas that jump into your mind as you work away at a project, make up a *Delegation Record*. Include vertical columns for tasks assigned, due date and date completed. Instead of interfering with your project and your employees, jot down the assignment or idea that came to you and get back to work. By the afternoon you may have accumulated a dozen or so items that you want to communicate to your staff. Cover them all in one sitting instead of one at a time as they occur. This eliminates those continual interruptions. Have a separate sheet for each person reporting to you, and get a commitment as to when each assignment is to be completed. Record it under the "due date." Now there's no danger of forgetting to follow up on all those assignments. Simply scan the sheet daily. Better still, put the due date in the follow-up section of your planner.

Have you ever made "spontaneous" assignments? For example, walking down a hallway, the sight of someone might remind you of a job you wanted them to do. "Oh, John", you'd say, "I just remembered. Could you get a quote for me on BlackBerrys for our staff? I need the cost for a report I'm writing."

"Sure, no problem", they'd answer. But you wouldn't hear from them. They would forget. Worse still, *you* might forget. And not until you decided to finish the report in time for the next day's meeting would you remember. This could happen with many of the verbal assignments you make. The people may not make a note of it, and neither may you. You'd both forget. When you

108

did remember (perhaps too late), and called about it, you would get responses such as, "Sorry, Jack. I've been terribly busy. But I have it on my list to do today", or "Funny you should call. I'm just working on it now." Would you believe it? Whenever you call to question a job that hasn't been completed yet, they are either working on it or about to work on it. Ever feel you're psychic? Imagine always calling at that precise moment after having forgotten about it for over a week!

Do you think they would have been "just working on it" if you had called three or four days earlier? Well, start using the *Delegation Record*; that's precisely what might happen. Each morning check the *Delegation Record* for any assignments due that day. Then phone right away. Don't wait until the day after the assignment is due and then ask if they have done it. Chances are they haven't done it or they'd have given it to you.

It only embarrasses the employee, since they have to admit they didn't do it and come up with excuses why they didn't. And it's already too late to get it on time, anyway. Instead, the morning of the due date say, "Bill, I realize it's early in the day, but I was just wondering if you anticipate any trouble getting that job to me today. You know, the printer paer useage summary?"

"Oh, no. No problem. In fact, I'm just working on it now." The same answer you would get if you didn't call until a week after it was due! They still may have forgotten it, but your call reminded them. They saved face. You get your project on time. Everybody's happy.

There's another advantage in using the *Delegation Record*. Whenever you asked them when they think they can get a task done, and you write down their answer, they will usually make a note as well. If you think it is

Exhibit 7

Delegation Record

MANAGER_____MONTH_____

Date Assigned	Assignment	Due Date	Date Completed	Comments

"INSTANT" TASKS   check box at right when completed

Form No. P3

important enough to write down, they think it is important as well. And consequently there will be less chance of them forgetting. You should make one thing clear to your staff; if they are unable to complete an assignment by the agreed upon date, they must let you know *before* the due date, not *after*. If everyone schedules tasks on a planning calendar well in advance, they should know in advance whether a task has to be rescheduled. Don't accept comments like, "I'm sorry, but things were really hectic last week so I couldn't get project 'A' done." Assuming you have negotiated a reasonable deadline, they should be able to say instead, "Things are really getting hectic this week; I don't think I'll be able to complete project 'A' by Friday as planned." Knowing in advance allows you to reschedule projects if the one due Friday is a priority. Or to advise your boss or customer of the change in plans, if it's not.

The form described here has a column for *Comments.* Use it if you want to keep track of your employee's performance. Was the job complete, well done, creative, submitted early or late, finished with the aid of others? This becomes a handy reference at performance appraisal time (Exhibit 7).

There is also an *Instant Tasks* section at the bottom of the form for those little tasks that only take a minute or two to complete, requests such as "check flight times," "write to Bob Wilson," "call printers re: lead time." It's not necessary to assign a deadline for these items. You expect them to be done that day or within a day or two at the most. Including them among the delegations will only clutter up the form. On a daily basis, when you are either making assignments or follow-ups, you would ask about these items, placing a check mark beside the items completed. This is a great place to jot down questions you want to ask people or things you want to tell them.

Don't lose sight of the fact that you may be the one who has to take action on some of those sudden inspirations. Schedule specific times for them in your time planner. The shorter *instant tasks* can be recorded as a *things to do* list in the same planner.

An added advantage of maintaining a *Delegation Record* is that it highlights how many tasks you are assigning to the various people reporting to you. You might be amazed at the number of jobs you are passing along to one person. Seeing the jobs in writing is a revelation. Because one particular person is reliable, never complains, or just can't say "no", she or he may be on the receiving end of most of your requests. You might have to change your ways in order to balance the workload. One thing we cannot afford to do as managers is to further develop our better people while ignoring the less skilled ones.

It's not only important to write things down, but to do it in an organized manner. Develop the habit of recording your calls, visits, assignments, and ideas that occur to you. Those two forms in a three-ring binder, combined with a daily planning calendar, will keep you from overlooking, misplacing or forgetting ideas, tasks and assignments that would put a strain on your effectiveness.

The Telephone & Visitor's Log and *Delegation Record* forms, placed in a binder with other relevant forms, will become your *Personal Organizer*.

Telephone Directory

Most people still keep business cards, even though they are quickly outdated and difficult to organize. Some people have a desk drawer filled with them, and think they're organized if they have them divided into piles with elastic bands around them! Can you imagine trying to find a specific card? They would play "search and find" every time they wanted to retrieve one. Then, once they had used it (unsuccessfully in many cases because people are always changing jobs), they would toss it back in the drawer and would waste more time later. Although you could scan cards into your computer or PDA as explained in alater chapter, some people prefer a hard copy directory.

To eliminate any hassle, draw up the *Telephone Directory* form which includes a column to record the type of business the person is in (or a physical description of the person). By adding a set of alphabetical tabs to the *Personal Organizer*, these sheets could be included in any quantity. If you run out of space under the 'A's or 'B's you need only add more sheets. If the directory becomes outdated you only have to copy over one page at a time. The *Telephone Directory* is always with you when you're talking on the telephone. Numbers can be transferred easily from the *Telephone & Visitor's Log* to the *Directory* (Exhibit 8).

But isn't a hard copy telephone directory a little old fashioned? There are PDAs, electronic directories, business card scanners, contact management software, and gadgets being developed almost weekly that will maintain your database in digital format. That's true, and if they are portable enough, easy to use, and faster, by all means use them. But some people insist they can flip

Exhibit 8

Telephone Directory

NAME / ORGANIZATION / ADDRESS	OTHER	CONTACT NUMBERS
		Business:
		Home:
		Fax:
		Mobile:
		E-mail:
		Business:
		Home:
		Fax:
		Mobile:
		E-mail:
		Business:
		Home:
		Fax:
		Mobile:
		E-mail:
		Business:
		Home:
		Fax:
		Mobile:
		E-mail:
		Business:
		Home:
		Fax:
		Mobile:
		E-mail:
		Business:
		Home:
		Fax:
		Mobile:
		E-mail:

Form No. P2

open an old fashioned hard copy directory to the right name faster than they can turn on or boot up an electronic marvel. But you have a choice. You can make up your own *Personal Organizer* using a three-ring binder, making up forms similar to those described, and buying dividers and alphabetical tabs from a stationery store. Or you can purchase one ready made.

Meeting Participant's Action Sheet

If you attend meetings, this is another useful form to add to your *Personal Organizer*. Use a *Meeting Participant's Action Sheet* to summarize the decisions reached, action required, whose responsibility it is to initiate the action, and the date that action is to be completed. With this summary sheet you won't have to wait for the minutes to arrive before you take action. You will also be able to spot any errors in the minutes. And if there are no minutes, these notes are a must. (See Exhibit 9.)

The *Meeting Participant's Action Sheet* will also enable you to keep the meeting on track even though you are not the chairperson. If you find the group discussing an agenda item before a decision was reached on a previous item, you can break in with "Excuse me, Jack, I didn't hear the decision reached on the previous item." Groups frequently drift to other topics inadvertently, and you can quickly bring this to their attention. A study conducted by R. M. Greene and Associates revealed that approximately 35 percent of topics discussed at meetings did not terminate in any action outcome. By being an active participant, you can help make the meeting more effective. If you have taken the time to attend the meeting, you owe it to yourself, and

Exhibit 9

Meeting Participants Action Sheet

NAME OF GROUP: _____ DATE: _____

IN ATTENDANCE: _____

AGENDA ITEM	DECISION REACHED	ACTION REQUIRED	PERSON RESPONSIBLE	COMPLETION DATE

© 1988 Harold Taylor Time Consultants Inc.

Form No. P5

116

to others to help make the meeting as productive as possible. Make sure you get your money's worth, because meetings are expensive.

By filling in the columns of the *Meeting Participant's Action Sheet* you can quickly tell whether any essential decisions were made (or not), what action is to be taken, the person responsible, and the date of completion. Ideally, everyone at the meeting should keep similar notes.

Don't rely on your memory

If you have ever forgotten to follow up on assignments, have interrupted your staff and peers several times a day, failed to take note of a telephone number or had a telephone request "slip your mind", develop or buy a *Personal Organizer*. You will eliminate a handful of time wasters. Don't rely on your memory and don't resort to scraps of paper. Make notes in an organized manner. Another section in my *Personal Organizer* contains lined note paper. I make notes at seminars, during interviews with clients, while cruising cyberspace, or during brainstorming sessions with my staff or myself. Here I keep records of quotes, web sites, media contacts, book ideas and anything that pops into my head that might be useful later. You can get in the habit of writing things down even if you don't have a *Personal Organizer*. Carry a pocket scratch pad or several index cards in your pocket or purse at all times. If you meet someone at a dinner party or get a brilliant idea while watching a soccer game, you can capture the idea immediately.

And don't forget to make maximum use of your time planner. Write as much information in it as possible, including names, addresses, phone numbers, locations, cities, hotels, materials required at meetings, flight numbers, restaurants visited. Enter special events such as birthdays, anniversaries, weddings. Flag them with small colored self-adhesive labels. Record those necessary but low priority "things to do" in the appropriate column. When you record a telephone call reminder, include the telephone number so it's easier to follow up later. Sketch maps of how to get to meetings in an unfamiliar location. Jot down expenses, mileage. The more information you are able to record, the more useful your time planner will be, both now and after the fact, when you want to recall where you've been, who you met, what you did, and how much you spent.

Writing things down increases your ability to concentrate as well as aids recall. Make notes at seminars, when being briefed by your boss, and when attempting to commit something to memory. Read with a highlighter in your hand and a pen within reach. Mark key words and passages, make marginal notes for later review. Never rely on your memory no matter how good you think it may be. Jot notes on incoming mail as thoughts occur to you. Write notations on the backs of business cards at the time they're given to you for later reference. Make notes when listening to CDs or watching a DVD. And keeping a diary or daily log is a terrific idea.

It's difficult to take notes while you're driving, but you can do just that if you get yourself a pocket recorder. If you're listening to an educational CD, for instance, simply stop the player when an idea strikes and record the thought.

Are you starting to feel a little more organized now?

If not, you've moved too quickly. Reread these first chapters. Take advantage of anything you feel will help you. Then put them into practice. The subsequent chapters will add icing to the cake. You will be able to refine your work habits and methods to increase your effectiveness even more. You will soon be managing yourself effectively with respect to time.

Chapter 8

Slay the paperwork dragon

Monitor the paperwork

Buck Rodgers explained in his book, *The IBM Way* (Harper & Row, 1986) that a few of the branch managers complained about the amount of paperwork crossing their desks. He asked the mailroom to send to him every piece of paper the branches were receiving. In a week, his desk was covered with so much material that there was no room for anything else. To ease the situation he ordered a control point where information was prioritized. The flow of unnecessary paperwork was curtailed and the number of people who could communicate directly with the branch offices was reduced.

Extending this idea, it might not be a bad idea to monitor for a week the paperwork being diverted to our employees' desks. Perhaps they are receiving magazines, reports, junk mail, and other paperwork that does nothing to increase their effectiveness. Sometimes we complain about the paperwork but we do nothing to curtail it.

For example, some people go overboard when subscribing to magazines. As a result, many of them pile up unread, taking valuable space, wasting time, and frustrating the subscribers. It is better to receive only a few, meaningful publications and read the relevant articles, than to suffer magazine overload and read next to nothing.

In spite of the expectations of computers and e-mail, paper is still a force to be dealt with. Experts have tabulated that North American office printers spewed out 1.2 trillion sheets of paper in 2001; an increase of 50 percent since 1996. (Managing Your E-Mail by Christina Cavanagh, John Wiley & Sons, 2003.) U.S.

Postal Services figures indicated that in 2003 more than 20 billion catalogs were mailed in the U.S. - the equivalent of 70 catalogs for every man, woman and child. (Source: The 60-Second Organizer by Jeff Davidson, Adams Media, 2004)

How many association rosters, catalogs, reports and periodicals do you have in your office? Make it a habit to toss the old copy when an updated one arrives. Many people accumulate clutter simply because they don't take the time to file things in an orderly way in the first place. Not wanting to waste time trying to find something in order to toss it, they simply keep the new copy as well. It's not unusual to find several back issues of resource books, magazines and reports that are no longer relevant. Clutter costs both time and money. Statistics reported in *Inc. Magazine* [May,1993] revealed that:

- 7.5 % of documents get lost completely
- 3% of the remainder get misfiled
- $120 in labor is spent finding a misfiled document
- $250 in labor is spent recreating a lost document.

Disorganization is expensive.

Declare war on paperwork

The war on paperwork has taken the form of the automated office. Companies are actually setting goals that include the virtual elimination of paperwork within five years. Although the goal may be unrealistic, it is a worthy one to aim for. And all companies should attempt to reduce paperwork through the use of imaging, electronic mail, voice mail and whatever technology is available.

But it is equally important that a person's *thinking* changes, not just his or her office equipment. One of the problems of communication is that there's simply too much of it. And if we make it easier to communicate, this problem will be magnified. Do copies, hard copy or electronic, have to be sent to everyone? Can distribution lists be reduced? Does everything have to be in writing? Do we need confirming letters, minutes, or action summaries before we actually do anything?

What happened to good old talking and listening? What's wrong with people making their own notes at meetings and marking commitments in their planner? What about verbal assignments recorded by the delegatee? Can we listen to reports on CDs? Telephone instead of write? Circulate instead of duplicate? Can we somehow escape the "put it in writing" mentality and put it into action instead?

I don't have the answers. But I do suggest that the evolution in technology should be matched with a revolution in thinking. We must escape the "protect my back" philosophy and replace it with an emphasis on trust, mutual respect, dependability, commitment, initiative. Managers must become goal-oriented and self-disciplined. And they must be evaluated more on what they accomplish and less on what they can verify in writing.

The tyranny of the in-basket

It's said that if a manager keeps busy enough he or she won't realize they're not accomplishing anything. And one thing that tends to keep a manager in perpetual motion is that bottomless receptacle called the in-basket.

For many of us that infernal in-basket commands our attention and detracts us from those priority goal-related activities. It attracts an endless array of paperwork emanating from others — memos, letters, reports, computer printouts, meeting notices, magazines, junk mail — randomly deposited by people passing by our desk.

Although I recommend that people ignore their mail until it's time to work on it, this is seldom done. Not only do most people snatch up paperwork the moment it appears, some actually abandon what they are working on in order to work on the distraction. Individuals with little self-control could actually work continually on incoming material, ignoring their own priorities in order to work on other peoples' priorities. Conceivably a person could remain busy all day working on items as they arrive, becoming a slave to his or her in-basket, with no time for planning or scheduling. Why do we succumb to the tyranny of the in-basket and how do we shake ourselves free? Here are a few observations and recommendations.

Curiosity. We lack self-discipline and our curiosity gets the best of us. "I wonder what that is?" We take a peek, which leads to time spent reading it and in some cases being side-tracked by it. Decide in advance when you will review the mail. Ignore it until that time. If the temptation is too great, move your in-basket out of sight, outside your office or in a spot where you can't reach it.

Lack of planning. Many managers don't have a daily plan, - a schedule of activities they will be working on. Consequently, they are easily sidetracked, looking to their in-basket for direction instead of their time planner or agenda. A "to do" list is not a plan. Determine your goals and schedule blocks of time to work on them. Deviate from that plan only to handle true emergencies.

Indecision. The in-basket never seems to empty. We review the paperwork, and if it is not urgent, we toss it back until it *becomes* urgent. We are forever digging into that in-basket, retrieving those urgent items. And the in-basket never seems to empty. When the time comes to review your mail, handle each piece of paper only once whenever possible. Never return it to the in-basket once you pick it up. Scrap it, do it, delegate it, file it or schedule time to do it later. Follow the 6 D's of mail handling described in Chapter 2. Take at least a half an hour each day to dispense with your mail. Indecision causes paperwork to accumulate. Don't procrastinate; when in doubt, toss it out.

If you have a computer on your desk and most of your "paperwork" is electronic, similar principles apply. Don't feel you instantly have to deal with everything that flashes on the screen, and be sure to schedule time for your priorities on your on-line planner before others zap meetings into all those open spaces. Develop the "do it now" habit when reviewing your electronic mail; don't retain everything - allow it to self-destruct or erase it immediately. We will discuss e-mail in the next chapter.

If you develop self-discipline and get in the habit of planning in order to accomplish those priority projects, and decide the disposition of a piece of paper whenever you pick it up, you will avoid the tyranny of the in-basket and manage your time more effectively.

Don't let paperwork get the best of you

A young lady attending my time management seminar reported using a self-inking stamp announcing "Deceased". She stamps all unwanted magazines, correspondence and junk mail and returns it to the senders. It no doubt drives marketers to a frenzy.

You may not want to follow her example. But one thing you should do is reduce the amount of paperwork you initiate. Paperwork breeds more paperwork, so think twice before putting things in writing. A telephone request will generally result in a telephone reply, but send a memo and you'll receive a memo in return. The *Telephone & Visitor's Log* described in Chapter 7, in which you summarize the telephone call, will serve as your written record should one be necessary.

If you feel you are required to issue a lot of unnecessary and time-consuming reports, calculate how much each report is actually costing. Issue the summary to your boss, asking whether he or she feels that they are worth the money. Sometimes people think differently once they realize a "nice to have" report is actually costing them $1,500 per year.

A study conducted by *Robert Half International* revealed that top executives spend 22 percent of their time writing or reading memos. Those polled (100 executives) felt that 39 percent of those memos are probably unnecessary. Although electronic mail is a great time saver, you can't beat *no* mail. Question the necessity of every memo you write. If you must write, do it as efficiently as possible. This could involve a little informality.

You could reduce paperwork by circulating memos, reports, etc., instead of making copies for everyone. Unfortunately, routing paperwork can be painfully slow, since people tend to hang onto it. One way of speeding up the process is to print up a routing slip with a message such as "It is imperative that this material be circulated promptly. Please read it immediately and place your signature and date opposite your name." As added insurance, always place the boss' name last.

Keep files thin

In some companies one might find thirty or forty copies of the same report, set of minutes, bulletin, memo or other piece of paper on permanent file. What a waste of time, money and space! The more paperwork that is filed away, the harder it is to retrieve anything. It would make more sense if one person were assigned the responsibility of filing his or her copy, while the others simply read theirs and discard it after taking the necessary action. If every department needs a copy of every report constantly at hand, perhaps the duplicate filing is necessary. But investigate. The thinner the files the more effective the organization.

Coping with the magazine explosion

Is your company inundated with magazines? Here are a few options to choose from:

Cancel subscriptions. Many people receive magazines by default. They fail to take the time to notify management that they don't need or want certain magazines. Ask each employee to list the titles of the magazines they want to continue receiving. Don't have them check them off a list or they'll check ones they don't need just to be on the safe side. If they can't recall what magazines they receive, they probably aren't having much of an impact on their effectiveness.

Receive one copy of each magazine and circulate it Multiple copies cause clutter, and since they don't have to be circulated, people have no sense of urgency to deal with them. Subscribe to one or two copies only, and circulate them to up to 10 people, along with an attached list of names so recipients can initial and date when they pass them on to the next person.

Photocopy the contents page of one copy and circulate the contents page only. People can check off the articles they are interested in reading. Photocopies are sent to them and they never have to spend time flipping through the magazines themselves and being distracted by interesting but useless articles, advertising or photos.

Distribute a list of magazines. In this case the company receives one copy only. It is filed in a central "library". A list of magazines available is distributed and the individuals check off which magazines they would like to see that month. The problem with this method is that most people check off more than they need for fear of missing something — and they have no idea what the magazines contain in the way of information that month.

If you do receive magazines it is imperative that you dispense with them as efficiently as possible. Here again, there are some options:

Schedule a reading time. Flipping through magazines at a set time each day or week will prevent them from accumulating.

Handle them as received. Some people treat magazines as any other piece of mail. Flipping to the contents page, identifying articles of interest, tearing them out and tossing them into a "To Read" folder, they do the actual reading during moments of idle time.

Guillotine the magazines. Removing the center staples and slicing the magazine down the center fold produces a stack of pages that could be flipped through easily — interesting items being retained..

Keep a reading file. A portable file or portfolio in your briefcase ensures that reading material is at hand for those unexpected delays such as waiting in lobbies, waiting for meetings to start, in restaurants, hotels, or subways.

Read smarter, not longer

If more magazines and books become electronic as expected, the paperwork problem should be reduced; but reading time will still be as scarce as ever. Above all, be selective in what you read. 80 percent of the value comes from 20 percent of the articles you read.

You certainly can't read everything. James T. McKay, in his book *The Management of Time,* suggests you can read 50,000 words a minute. All you have to do is recognize within one minute that a 50,000-word book is not going to help you and then don't read it! How long do you spend reading magazines? Some people subscribe to as many as 15 magazines and actually spend time with all of them. If a magazine doesn't consistently offer articles of interest, get off the circulation list. Resist the temptation to accept them simply because they're free. Read only those magazines and books that will help you attain your self-development goals. One or two useful articles a year is not sufficient payback for your time invested.

How you read is important as well. Read actively. The average reading speed is only 230 to 250 words a minute. But you can scan literature at 1,000 to 5,000 words a minute. Don't simply absorb whatever information hits your eye. Search out the information you require. The title should tell you what the article is about. Turn it into a question and actively search for the answers. For example, if the article is entitled "How to save time at meetings", change it to read "How can I save time at meetings?" and search for those sentences that provide the information you're looking for. By reading with a purpose, your mind will not wander and you'll cover the material more quickly. Even the process of holding the highlighter in your hand as you read will make it easier to concentrate. It makes you a more active participant in the reading and improves recall later.

Everyone wants to keep current. But with thousands of magazines to choose from, and with managers already spending over thirteen hours a week reading business-related material, we must have a strategy in order to manage our time effectively in this area.

Cruising the Internet

There's so much to read on the internet, you could cruise forever, and that's the problem. People can become addicted to endlessly clicking windows and sorting through data and "surfing the net." It's important from a time perspective to limit yourself to those benefits which produce maximum return. The old 80-20 rule applies to electronic communications as well; 80 percent of the results can be achieved by taking advantage of only 20 percent of the available services. Be selective in what your read and/or download.

If you visit web sites that are of interest, be sure to bookmark them for later reference.

While browsing the web you might also encounter information that you want to record, so make up electrnic folders titled with the topics of interest to you. Cut and paste information, along with the source,from websites you visit and file them in these folders. As far as interesting places to visit are concerned, there are plenty. But limit yourself to those sites that provide the information you need. For example, if you need to find a company address or telephone number, *Big Book* has 16 million U.S. addresses on line. Look up the company by name or by type of business. It will even provide a map and directions to get there if you need them. [*www.bigbook.com.*] If you need information on a company, try contacting *Hoover's Handbook* at *www.hoovers.com.* Useful advice for business people is available at *Idea Site for Business* at *www.ideasitefor-*

business.com. It includes information on marketing products, articles on getting organized and a list of 103 marketing ideas. If you want to refer to newspapers, *Editor and Publisher* is a data-base directory of 1610 online newspapers from around the world. Those in Canada and the U.S. are broken down by Province and State respectively. [*www.mediainfo.com.*

If you want to know if a flight is on time before you leave for the airport to meet it, check out *at http://travel.airwise.com/arrivals.*

If you're traveling to another country, you might want to contact the *Universal Currency Converter* site at *www.xe.net/currency/.*

\ The Internet and its service providers have made research much faster and less expensive. Want to access articles on time management, marketing, promotion and other business topics? Contact Arcamax Publishing (ezines@arcamax.com) for a continuing supply. Other time management articles can be downloaded from my website at *www.taylorintime.com.*

Another useful web site, produced by professional speakers Rebecca Morgan and Ken Braly is located at http://www.speakernetnews.com/. Here you will find a collection of tips on topics such as technology, travel and opportunities in the speaking business, most submitted by professional speakers who receive the weekly electronic newsletter.

If you want to discuss problems with others, enter one of the chat rooms. *Home Office Computing* has its own chat room, but there are dozens of others. You can even form your own special interest group, create your own chat room, and discuss topics of mutual interest. But limit the time you spend cruising cyberspace. Know what you're looking for and don't be sidetracked by interesting but irrelevant information. And don't add to the paperwork explosion by printing documents unless you need them in hardcopy form.

When you write, write right

Since you will never be able to completely avoid writing , your next challenge is to be informal, courteous and brief. Don't stuff your sentences with big words, unnecessary adjectives, and ambiguous phrases. Don't waste time searching for the "right" words. Memos tend to become wordy, formal and frequently unintelligible. Remember that the objective of a memo or letter is to communicate, not to impress. Try to retain your own personality. Be simple. Informal. Natural. And come to the point quickly.

Don't get hung up on grammar or vocabulary. The trend is towards informality and no one will ridicule you for starting a sentence with "and" or leaving out the odd verb or even for allowing a participle or two to dangle. It's more important to have your letters carry that personal touch. To have them capture the reader's attention. And to write with the reader's wants and needs in mind.

This doesn't mean you should use poor grammar intentionally. Standard English gives a greater assurance that you and your reader will be on the same wavelength. But acceptable business style is literate, not literary. Ostentation or pomposity *does not* impress. It only arouses suspicion in the mind of the reader.

Here are a few suggestions to keep your memos and e-mail messages brief, natural, *and* more effective:

Keep your sentences short.

It's okay to have a long one now and then. In fact it breaks the monotony. But keep them separated with lots of short, simple sentences.

Use familiar, simple words.

Instead of searching for long words, designed to impress, try looking for short ones or two-syllable words to substitute for the long ones. And stay away from jargon.

Use verbs in the active voice.

Don't say "It was decided at a meeting of the board of directors..." Try instead, "The board of directors decided..." Using the active voice makes your letters come alive. And cuts down the word count.

Avoid tiresome expressions.

Be original. Stay away from expressions like "a few well-chosen words," "assuring you of our prompt attention," or "attached please find." Most expressions of this type can be eliminated altogether.

Be direct.

Don't use two or three words when one will do: "at your earliest convenience" is "soon"; "due to the fact that" is "because." See Exhibit 10 for more examples of keeping your writing brief.

Use adjectives sparingly.

Stay clear of those senseless, unnecessary adjectives that add nothing to the meaning: for example, "*practical* experience" (is there any other kind?) and "establish *necessary* criteria" (would anyone want to establish *unnecessary* criteria?)

Write in the first person.

You wouldn't talk on the phone that way, so why write that way? "I hear" is a lot more natural and more simple than "It was brought to my attention." And it requires fewer words.

It's oversimplifying things to say "write like you talk." When we talk we usually keep repeating ourselves and that just isn't necessary when writing. To become an effective writer you have to work at it. Keep asking yourself if that adjective is necessary, or whether there's a shorter way of saying something. With practice you will be able to write effectively using only half as many words. That saves time for you *and* the reader.

Keep business reports business-like.

Keep your reports short. Your solution to the problem, and your recommendations, are what people want, not your play by play description of everything that happened. Business reports should not read like suspense novels. Be direct. Keep them simple. Be brief. Sure, you put a lot of time and effort into your investigation, but why take it out on the reader? Summarize the conclusions and recommendations on the first page. Let them read about your reasoning and all your work later, if they have time. And tack all those detailed statistics, charts and graphs on the end as an addendum. Always keep in mind that you're being paid for results, not words.

Exhibit 10

Keep Your Writing Brief

Instead of this	Say this
in the majority of instances	most often or usually
in a number of cases	frequently or some
on a few occasions	occasionally or sometimes
the only other alternative	the alternative
I would appreciate you informing me	please tell me
at your earliest convenience	soon
due to the fact that	because
for the month of July	for July
in compliance with your request	as requested
in a satisfactory manner	satisfactorily
in view of the fact that	as
notwithstanding the fact that	although
I wish to apologize	I apologize
in the near future	soon
in the amount of	for
enclosed please find	enclosed
at the present time	now
this is to thank you	thank you
in the event that	if
after very careful consideration	after considering
in order to	to
will hold a meeting	will meet
in view of the above	for these reasons
at that point in time	then
as of this date	today, to date or now
during the time that	while
from the commercial standpoint	commercially
had occasion to be	was
in this day and age	today
made an approach to	approached
made a statement saying	said
retain position as	remain
take action on the issue	act

was of the opinion that	thought or believed
was witness to	saw
at this juncture in time	now
in the neighborhood of	about
caused injuries to	injured
are present in greater abundance	are more abundant
am in possession of	have
bound and determined	determined
why in the world	why
a substantial segment of the population	many people
fully cognizant of	know well
ahead of schedule	early
take into consideration	consider
in the event that	if
along the lines of	like
for the purpose of	for
the reason that	because
in the case of	if
on the grounds that	since
with reference to	about
with the result that	so that
one and the same	the same
had intended to	meant
I deem it advisable	it's advisable
it's with considerable pleasure	I'm happy to
afford an opportunity	allow
at all times	always
experience has indicated that	we have learned
meets with our approval	we approve
subsequent to	after

Chapter 9

Writing, sending & receiving effective e-mail

Advantages of e-mail

Compared to the process of typing a letter, printing and folding it, placing it in an envelope, applying postage and mailing it, e-mail is an electronic marvel. And it comes at a time when time itself is at a premium. Anything that carves precious minutes from an activity or task is welcomed with open arms. But the advantages do not stop there. It is generally much easier to write an e-mail message than a letter. The signature is automatic, a full salutary address is often not needed and the letter is addressed with the click of a mouse. The message is delivered, in most cases, instantaneously. It goes around the world without postage and can be sent simultaneously to hundreds of people. There are no envelopes to be opened and discarded, no mess, no paperwork of any kind. It's easily filed, deleted, forwarded or printed. A response can be sent immediately by merely clicking the Reply button. Any portion of the original letter can be left intact for clarification when answering questions. Assuming you have a laptop or home computer, messages can be written and sent at anytime of the day or night. In fact with a laptop or PDA messages can be sent and received while traveling. Add a cellular telephone or wireless PDA and you can write letters at a ballpark or in a moving vehicle. Incoming messages can be filtered, sorted and filed with ease. No visible filing cabinets or storage boxes are needed. No tangible in baskets or file folders. No staples, paper clips or 3 hole punches. Simple, fast and environmentally friendly.

Sounds great. But that's just the beginning. E-mail also provides an alternative to those incessant phone calls that interrupt you at inopportune times or clog up your voice mailbox. E-mail can be sent and received at any time at your convenience. It eliminates time zone problems and long distance charges. No more telephone tag. And no more listening to messages to determine their importance. Subject lines and addresses allow you to delete e-mail unopened.

If you leave a voice mail message and send an e-mail message, the latter will probably be answered first. It's easier for the receiver to click Reply then to make a phone call. It also allows simultaneous communications. If you're away from the office, you don't have to phone in for your e-mail messages, you can access them from any computer, BlackBerry or other handheld device.

No wonder e-mail is rapidly replacing business letters. The advantages are awesome. So why all the complaints about e-mail?

Disadvantages of e-mail

The fact that e-mail is so easy to send and possesses all these advantages is the reason it is causing problems for most people. Wayne McKinnon's Complete Guide to E-Mail states that millions of people from Fortune 500 businesses to small enterprises to individuals use e-mail daily in place of telephone calls, faxes, courier shipments and letter mail. Advantages can become disadvantages in the hands of someone who uses it carelessly. E-mail is being used when it isn't needed. It is being sent to people who don't want it. It is being used to replace face-to-face contact. People a few feet from each other in offices are exchanging every joke, story or anecdote that comes their way. People are being copied indiscriminately. The fact that it's easy encourages its overuse.

Too many messages are being sent to too many people, too often, with too many people being copied, using too many words with too many mistakes and too little forethought. Many e-mailers write carelessly, with little heed for grammar or typos. They use incomplete sentences, little punctuation and rambling sentences. Thus another disadvantage looms - miscommunication.

The advantages of e-mail are phenomenal. But to take advantage of the advantages, organizations must develops policies and procedures, instigate training programs and help employees streamline their writing skills. In their zeal to save time and take advantage of technology, businesses seem to have thrown out the baby with the bath water. The bath water is the hard copy letters that we used to write. The baby is the effective writing itself.

E-mail is on the increase.

In 1998, e-mail surpassed the telephone as the most frequently used communication medium in the office, claimed an article in the Wall Street Journal. In 1999, 536 billion e-mails were sent in the U.S. alone, compared with 206 billion pieces of snail mail according to the April 2001 issue of Home Office Computing. A University of California-Berkeley study estimated e-mails during 2001 at 600 billion to 1.1 trillion. (St. Petersburg Times, March 5, 2001.) Christina Cavanagh, in her book Managing Your E-Mail (John Wiley & Sons, 2003) says that North Americans receive an average of 48 e-mails per day. Leslie Bendaly, author of Winner Instinct (HarperCollins, 1999,) says that she has met people who sort through more than one hundred e-mails daily. Others have quoted even higher figures.

A poll of 26 top executives, conducted by Spencer Stuart's Chicago office, revealed that 76 percent of them spent at least one hour each day reading and responding to e-mail, with 12 percent spending more than three hours per day. (Management Review, September, 1999.) Almost everyone in my time management workshops claim they spend over one hour per day reading and responding to e-mail and that the amount of time spent is increasing every year.

A 2002 study predicted that we would soon be spending more than 4 hours each day reading and answering fifty work-related messages. Cavanagh claims that e-mail has lengthened the workday by about one hour. In spite of its timesaving qualities, e-mail, can become a timewaster itself if not managed properly.

Schedule time for e-mail.

Don't interrupt yourself by continually checking your e-mail throughout the day. 79% of users look at their messages as soon as they receive them. Continual interruptions such as those play havoc with your effectiveness. Delete obvious spam without opening them. The subject lines reveal a lot about the content. Have specific mail times such as first thing in the morning and again after lunch. Checking messages at the end of the day is probably not a good idea since there's no time to take action. And you'll catch the mail in the morning anyway. Never check e-mail until you have time to deal with it. Dispense with messages one at a time. Delete, file, respond or forward them. If they represent long-term tasks, transfer the needed information to your planner and delete or archive the messages.

Generally, the same principles apply to electronic mail as hard copy mail when it comes to dispensing with it. Once you have scheduled time to handle it, do it, delegate it, delete it, file it or arrange for it to be done later. It's important to control your in-basket.

Keep e-mail to a minimum.

When an incoming e-mail message merits a thank you, say little else. Don't add unnecessary comments that might encourage another reply in return. There is too much e-mail that simply serves to thank others for thanking them. "You're welcome" is usually unnecessary. Don't feel compelled to get in the last word.

Don't clutter your electronic files with non-essential correspondence. Delete most e-mail and only file those that you have to refer to in the future. Print as few as possible and don't keep both printed and electronic versions. According to a survey conducted by Dianna Booher, of all the documents that are printed, copied and distributed by North American business every day, 75 to 80 percent are never referred to again. E-mail loses much of its advantage if it is printed. Yet, according to an article in the Stouffville Tribune (Just Delete the Frustrations of E-Mail, by Arthur Black,) 60 percent of all e-mail is still copied onto paper. Resist the urge to print your e-mail. Answer it, file it, or delete it. But don't keep it unless absolutely necessary.

Keep the reader in mind.

When sending e-mail, respect other people's time as well. Before you send that message to your entire mailing list, ask yourself a question. Would you send that many copies if it were paperwork? Send it only to those who need it or can benefit from it. Don't let the circulation list be determined by the ease of transmission.

Use a relevant header to make it easy to file. If you're replying to a message and changing the topic, take a few seconds to change the subject line to correspond with the new topic. Make sure the header grabs the reader's attention and immediately identifies the topic. The only way some people can cope with the overload of e-mail is to delete most unsolicited messages unread. They make this decision based on the header. A vague title such as "Opportunity" or "Thought you might be interested" could easily be deleted accidentally. If the receiver knows you, you might want to include your name in the header. And if you're replying to their e-mail, say so. Avoid attachments and graphics that slow e-mail downloading.

Keep e-mail business-like.

Although e-mail is sometimes viewed as a casual, conversational form of communication, it is rapidly becoming the accepted form of business communication as well. As such it warrants similar guidelines to that of hardcopy correspondence. Keep your message brief and indicate any action you want the reader to take. Limit each message to one topic. Use the Spell Checker feature; careless typing and sloppy grammar will reflect on both you and your company. Assume that all your e-mail will be saved and viewed by others. Formality is even more important when corresponding to people in other countries who may not be accustomed to the more casual approach to communication.

There are dozens of symbols called emoticons representing the various emotions such as happiness, sadness etc., and even more acronyms that people seem to be using, but I don't recommend either. Everyone is not familiar with them. Personally, I get annoyed when I encounter such hieroglyphics as LOL, IMHO, IMHO or OTOH. It may save the writer a few seconds, but I waste my time trying to figure out what the gobbledygook means. We survived quite nicely in the days of hardcopy letters without smiles, frowns and laughter symbols plastered in our letters. Why the necessity now?

Watch the format.

H. Block and Jeff Senne, in their book, CyberPower for Business (Book-mart Press, 1996,) point out that computer screens are shorter than sheets of paper, so the most important information should be in the header and first paragraph or two of the message, where it is in full view. They say you can figure on about twenty lines of message.

A signature file, which could include your name, company, telephone number, fax number, website address and one-line description of your business can be added automatically with most e-mail programs. It's unobtrusive at the end of the message, helpful to the reader and it compensates for the lack of a letterhead.

E-mail is one of the greatest timesaving marvels of the century. It takes about 30 minutes to write and send a business letter compared to 5 minutes to write and send an equivalent e-mail message, according to the book, E-mail @ Work by Jonathan Whaler. But it can also be a time waster to others if they receive needed and unwanted information. If misused it can be as much a hindrance as help. Use it, but don't abuse it.

Don't hide behind e-mail.

E-mail should enhance, not replace, personal communication. Don't use it to create a wall between you and your staff or to skirt around issues that should be tended to immediately. Keep the usual lines of communication open, including telephone calls and personal contact. Some things simply shouldn't be handled by e-mail. You wouldn't use it to discipline employees, deliver bad news, and communicate confidential information or for anything else that you would not want to be seen by others. As Nancy Friedman, known as the Telephone Doctor, says, "You are better off not putting anything in E-mail that you wouldn't want in tomorrow's newspaper."

One thing that e-mail should be used for according to Marilynne Ruddick and Leslie O'Flahaven, in their article, E-mail for Good, Not Evil (T+D, May 2001) is to give praise. It's common sense to congratulate staff at the time of their accomplishment, and the writers claim that it's one way to get your staff to read their mail. Certainly nobody should mind if those e-mails fall into the hands of the public!

Consider professional help.

E-mail is on the increase. And although it can be a great time saver, if mismanaged, it can also be a time waster. Consider having a consultant or professional organizer review your current procedures and guidelines to ensure that everyone in the organization is using it as effectively as possible.

E-mail: an overview.

It is imperative that everyone in the organization learns to write effectively with the reader in mind. Messages should be crisp, clear and concise. The following suggestions, in the form of an acronym spelling the word EMAIL, will provide a guideline for improving electronic communications.

Edit the message before you send it. The reputation of the organization is at stake. Speediness does not justify sloppiness. Use upper and lower case. Punctuate properly. Double-space paragraphs. Communicate clearly, indicating the action that you want the reader to take. Be professional. Avoid sexist language. Be sensitive to cultural differences. Don't write emotionally charged e-mails that you might later regret. And remember that there's no such thing as confidential e-mail. Don't say anything in your message that you wouldn't want the whole world to see.

Make your writing live. Let a positive attitude permeate your message. Be brief, but neither blunt nor boring. Avoid the passive voice, clichés, jargon, acronyms and gobbledygook. Avoid needless modifiers, wordy phrases, overused modifiers and long rambling sentences. Use action verbs. Vary the length of sentences. Separate paragraphs by double spacing. Double space and number any points being made. And keep the message to one screen if possible. Write to express, not to impress.

Always add any attachments before you address the e-mail. Most people have forgotten to include the attachment at one time or another. Guard against an itchy trigger finger by writing the e-mail before it is addressed. This will also give you the opportunity to edit the message before sending it. If the attachment is large, zip it and summarize the contents in the e-mail itself. Where possible, stay away from attachments altogether. Cut and paste the information into the e-mail. Viruses have made people reluctant to open attachments.

Identify yourself and the topic up front. Set your options so your full name and e-mail address appear in the From line. Use a subject line that accurately identifies the topic of the e-mail. And put the most important information in the first paragraph. Your objective is to get the reader to open your e-mail, read it and act upon it. With about 30% of e-mail being spam, this isn't easy. You run the risk of having your message deleted unopened if the header doesn't grab their attention. Indicate in the subject line whether the message is urgent or a priority, but use the word Urgent sparingly.

Limit each e-mail message to one topic only. You will have less problem writing a descriptive subject line and the message will be easier to file. It may also get a faster response. If people don't have all the answers to your questions they usually hold back until they do. Break up topics into separate e-mails and give them opportunities for immediate responses. You will also be able to pinpoint who should receive copies. Address the e-mail to the person who should respond, and copy everyone else.

Resist the urge to shoot off an e-mail when a telephone call or personal visit would be more appropriate. E-mail should enhance, not replace personal communication. Eighty-one percent of managers in one survey indicated that e-mails were being sent when personal communications would be more effective. Don't let the advantages of e-mail be offset by the many abuses that are possible.

Sending e-mail: a checklist

With e-mail rapidly becoming the most popular method of communication, it is important to become as efficient as possible while retaining clarity of purpose. Here is a list of suggestions for writing and sending e-mail. Check off those that make sense to you and implement them immediately.

Limit each e-mail message to one topic only. It makes it easier to file under a specific topic and retrieve later. It will usually result in a faster response to your message as well.

Use a heading that reveals the purpose of the message and grabs the reader's attention. You want to motivate the receiver to open your e-mail message rather than to delete it.

If you don't need a response, preface the subject line with FYI ONLY.
If it's urgent or a priority, say so; but use those words sparingly.

For brief messages consider including the entire message in the subject line.

Try to limit your message to one screen, about 25 lines of text.

Using the receipt function is generally a waste of time and might be considered an invasion of privacy.

Set your options so your full name and e-mail address appear in the from line for instant identification.

Address your e-mail with the recipient's name as well as their e-mail address. This is particularly helpful to all the people you CC.

For more formal business e-mails, include a salutation and close, such as Dear Mr. Smith and Yours sincerely.

When sending e-mail to a group, BCC everyone to keep the file size down. You may not want to reveal your mailing list to everyone, nor force them to scroll past a bunch of addresses to get to your message.

Start the message with the recipient's name.

If you're writing to a stranger, identify yourself up front.

Stay away from attachments where possible. Cut and paste shorter documents into the message section instead.

When you do include an attachment, do so before addressing the e-mail so you won't forget to attach it.

Zip large files before attaching them to speed up delivery and reduce download time.

For large attachments, summarize the contents in the e-mail message..

Don't put anything in an e-mail that you wouldn't want to have circulated to others.

Lead with the most important information. Put the most important information in the first paragraph (Inverted pyramid technique.)

Double space and number the points being made.

Don't cut corners by using all lower case letters. And definitely don't use all caps. It's not only considered shouting, it makes the memo more difficult to read.

brief. Use short sentences of 15 words or less and short paragraphs.

Don't flame or send emotionally charged messages.

Avoid plagiarism or illegal use of copyrighted material.

Avoid sexist language.

Be sensitive to cultural differences. For example, Americans read 6/10/03 as June 10th. Europeans read it as October 6th. Also watch the slang, use of humor and terminology.

Don't send confidential or private information via e-mail.

Don't use e-mail for personal solicitations at work. In fact, don't send any personal e-mail from work.

Ask your friends and associates for permission before you add them to any mailing list.

Don't use e-mail when another method of communication would be more appropriate.

Don't use abbreviations, jargon, acronyms or emoticons.

Write in the active voice.

Use good grammar and correct punctuation.

Separate paragraphs with spaces.

Keep lines less than 80 characters in length, preferably 65 to 70.

Write with the reader's interests in mind.

Be specific in telling the reader what you want them to do.

Break up long messages with headings.

When writing emotionally charged e-mail, leave it in your outbox overnight and read it again before sending it.

Review and edit all messages before sending them.

Your signature file is the equivalent of your letterhead. It should not run more than 6 to 8 lines. Include your name, company, address, telephone, fax, website and e-mail. But don't write a signature that looks like a promotional brochure.

Make it clear what action you want the reader to take. And specify a due date.

Develop a policy manual so employees will have guidelines for handling e-mail.

Collect samples of well-written e-mail and post them on the company intranet.

E-mail is not always urgent. Don't get tied up in knots by all the e-mail you receive. Sure, e-mail is a little more urgent than paper; many people use it to replace a telephone call. But people should not mind waiting a few hours to receive a reply. If it were that urgent, they would have called you anyway. So don't feel you have to reply the minute you receive it. Some people receive more than 100 messages a day, and they'd get little else done if they treated every message as though it were urgent.

Don't allow messages to accumulate. Handle them and get rid of them. Having set times each day to respond to e-mail is a good idea. Don't allow e-mail to interrupt you when you're working on a priority project. If a beep keeps reminding you that e-mail has been received, turn it off.

In the past, many of us used to take briefcases full of paperwork home with us. If we now take home laptops filled with e-mail, have we really progressed much? Technology is supposed to make life easier for us, not more hectic. Make sure everyone in the office is familiar with any new equipment and software, particularly the e-mail program you are using. If necessary, have the vendor conduct a training session with the staff. Technology is of little use if people don't take advantage of it.

Although many e-mail programs will include the original message when you click Reply, this is usually a nuisance to the reader. If necessary, add a few words to identify the e-mail that you're answering. At the most, leave a few of the sender's original words intact. In most cases even this is unnecessary since you have identified what you are responding to in the subject line. As Maureen Chase and Sandy Trupp point out in their book, Office E-mails That Really Click, when you return a person's telephone call you don't first repeat word for word the message they left on your voice mail. So why do it in e-mail?

Receiving e-mail.

If your organization doesn't rely on e-mail to a great extent in order to carry on business, checking e-mail twice per day is good enough. But if you rely on e-mail extensively, it should be checked about every hour. Here is a checklist of suggestions for handling incoming e-mail.

Have set times to review e-mail.

Check all the e-mails from one person before responding to any.

Don't reply to everything.

Turn off any alarm features.

Delete, reply, forward or file; don't delay.

File relevant parts only.

Expand window to full size for reading.

Don't print messages if avoidable.

Use the auto reply feature when away from the office.

Use the reply to all button sparingly.

Delegate where possible.

Have an organized filing system.

The evolution of Spam.

At first, we only had to cope with junk mail. It wasn't that intrusive. It was easily identified and could be discarded unopened. Many people actually liked receiving it. I suppose it was better than getting no mail at all. A survey conducted over twenty years ago revealed that 63% of the people looked forward to receiving it. 75% of the people even read the political mailings they received. I remember reading about one gentleman who relied on all the junk mail to heat his home. He tried to get onto everybody's mailing list.

Then junk telephone calls came on the scene and people weren't quite as receptive. The unsolicited calls interrupted them at inconvenient times, such as during family dinner. This was back in the days when families actually ate together. As technology improved, junk mail escalated and more devious tactics were used to ensure that you actually opened these unsolicited envelopes. Some disguised them as personal letters. Others deceived us into thinking they contained critical information. Some looked like telegrams, government correspondence, unpaid invoices or announcements that you had just won big sums of money. As junk mail increased, marketers became more creative, adding personalized envelopes and contents, real stamps, return postage, teaser copy, handwritten messages and dated material. Junk mail was becoming a nuisance.

Then came fax machines and with them, junk faxes. Fax broadcasting became big business. If people resented telephone solicitations, they hated unsolicited faxes. After all, some victims claim, the marketer is using our paper and our fax machines to advertise their product at a time convenient to them, regardless of whether we have any interest in the material or not. This form of junk mail escalated annually to the point where last year one Toronto company transmitted 75 million pages of fax documents across North America.

Meanwhile, as computers became commonplace and the Internet became a popular method of communicating, unsolicited e-mail, known as Spam, added to the junk mail pollution. Since electronic mail was inexpensive and easy to send, sheer volume became overwhelming. People were even less receptive to this electronic junk mail. It was not only intrusive and disruptive, but consumed large amounts of precious time. One study estimated the worldwide cost of Spam at more than $ 9 billion a year in online connection time alone. (More Than an Annoyance by Dave Gussow, St. Petersburg Times, March 5, 2001.) Spammers using software robots can collect e-mail addresses from websites, e-mail directories, bulletin boards etc. and sell lists to others for the purposes of sending unsolicited advertisements. Some advertisers are adept at disguising the header to imitate personal messages to get you to open them. An IMT Strategies survey found that 60 percent of the respondents felt negative about Spam. The Coalition Against Unsolicited E-mail (CAUCE) reported almost 95 percent of recipients didn't want to receive unsolicited messages. Here again, marketers were creative, disguising commercials as personal messages. Although up to 40 percent of e-mail messages may be Spam, there's always the fear of deleting something important.

Delete the obvious. Most Spam is easily identifiable without opening it. If the subject line is all in caps or contains exclamation marks or makes a sales pitch it's probably Spam. Sometimes the address of the sender is a dead giveaway, and so is the mention of $$ and savings and free offers and enticements too good to be true. If there is no heading at all, or one in a foreign language or one that's cut off because it's too long, it's likely spam.

Ways to reduce spam

Set up filters that will automatically delete or shuttle to a file folder those messages that meet certain criteria.

Don't respond to spam or you will simply verify your e-mail address.

Use a second e-mail address for ordering products, registering, subscribing, posting messages or any other activity that might result in being added to a mailing list.

To file a complaint direct a message to the postmaster@thatparticulardomain.com or replace everything before the @ with the word "abuse" before sending it to the service provider. For example, abuse@compuserve.com.

When replying to e-mail: a checklist

When replying to e-mail, keep the header relevant. Don't leave it at Thanks, for example, if you're onto another topic.

When forwarding messages, put your comments at the top of the message.

Don't continue to include the CCs if messages have become two-way communications.

Have boilerplate responses under appropriate headings for copying and pasting for answers to routine questions.

Only include enough of the original message to clarify which message you're responding to.

If the e-mail requires a response, reply even if you don't have the whole answer yet. Tell the sender when you will be able to provide a complete answer.

Chapter 10

The enemies of time management

Recognize your major time wasters

Ask people what their major time waster is and most of them will lead you to believe it is *other people.* "Constant interruptions," they'll tell you; "Employees constantly making mistakes"; or, "All those meetings I have to attend."

Don't you believe it. *We* are the ones primarily responsible for our own time management problems. And if you're going to be successful at managing yourself with respect to time, you will have to accept that fact - and do something about it. Exhibit 11 lists 64 time wasters that are entirely or partially within your control. Doesn't leave much, does it? I guarantee that if you reduce the time wasters that are within your control, the other ones will be unable to curb your effectiveness.

Most of them will be eliminated by proper organization, systems, procedures, and self-discipline. But a few involve breaking bad habits which you have acquired over the years. The more insidious ones that constantly plague managers will be dealt with in this chapter.

Procrastination, our biggest enemy

Someone said "Procrastination is the thief of time." It robs us of valuable time, keeps us disorganized, and leads to interruptions, crises, and stress.

Once we get hooked on procrastination, we find plenty of ways to support the habit. It's fed by the many excuses for delay, such as shuffling paperwork, straightening our desk, sorting through the mail or engaging in idle conversation. Procrastination is a parasite eating away at our effectiveness as managers. We must understand why and how it operates and eliminate it.

Exhibit 11

Common Time Wasters

1. Lack of delegation on your part or on the part of your supervisor
2. Procrastination: delaying distasteful or overwhelming tasks
3. Not scheduling priority tasks in your planner
4. Trouble getting started in mornings
5. Over-extended coffee breaks & lunches
6. Excessive idle time, talk, daydreaming
7. Sorting & dispensing with mail throughout the day
8. Searching for files, information
9. Reading magazines during prime time at office or home
10. Shuffling papers, searching for items on a cluttered desk
11. Proofreading and signing letters unnecessarily
12. Constant checking on employees
13. Spending too much time on non-priority items
14. Inter-office travel, visiting people unnecessarily
15. Too long on telephone
16. Re-writing memos & letters
17. Sleeping longer than necessary
18. Lack of written goals, no clear-cut objectives
19. Inability to say "no"
20. Holding unnecessary meetings
21. Poor control of meetings: Late starting, too long, getting sidetracked, etc.
22. Relying on mental notes, not writing things down
23. Circulating 'junk mail" (the paperwork game)
24. No "quiet hour", allowing continual interruptions
25. Not using prime time for priority work
26. Not utilizing waiting time, travel time, commuting time
27. Filing too much, throwing out too little
28. Self-interruptions, and interrupting others frequently
29. Not utilizing forms, form letters, model letters
30. Indecision, spending time on trivial decisions
31. Keeping separate "things to do" lists
32. Writing when a phone call would do
33. Inefficient office layout
34. Having separate planners for business & home
35. Not keeping secretary/assistant advised of appointments, meetings
36. Not having facts, telephone numbers readily at hand

37. Unclear communications or lack of communications
38. Not taking advantage of time-saving gadgets, equipment, supplies
39. Too much attention to detail; perfectionism
40. No weekly plan: reacting instead of planning
41. No self-imposed deadlines
42. Leaving tasks unfinished & starting new ones
43. Allowing upward delegation
44. Failure to reconfirm appointments
45. Not properly training staff
46. Firefighting - jumping from crisis to crisis
47. Preoccupation with problems, worry, anxiety, stress
48. Not using a follow-up system
49. Not actively listening
50. Too much time on personal & outside activities
51. Poor attitude toward the job
52. Lack of confidence, reluctance to try new methods
53. Lack of procedures, job descriptions, guidelines
54. Keeping items no longer used (packrat)
55. Poor writing skills, overly long letters or reports
56. Absentmindedness, forgetfulness
57. Allowing business cards to accumulate
58. Having more than one "junk drawer"
59. Writing messages, notes, on scraps of paper
60. Visiting or shouting to co-workers instead of using intercom
61. Continually taking work home with you
62. Stashing material under desk, on window ledges
63. Having a disorganized briefcase
64. Insufficient supply of pens, paper clips, etc. at your desk.

Procrastination is really *the intentional and habitual postponement of some important task that should be done now.* Any time you make a decision to do something at a specific time in the future, you are not procrastinating, you are planning. But if the postponement is habitual, i.e. you put it off until the next day, and then the next day, and then the next, and it's not merely a case of forgetting or being coerced into ignoring it, you're procrastinating. And it's still procrastination regardless of the excuses you have or the rationalizations you make for putting it off.

That's why procrastination is such an insidious time waster. It's deceitful. We make it look like we don't have time to do it, or that it makes sense to polish off the small tasks first to get them out of the way, or that we're saving time in the event that the boss changes his or her mind, or that the urgency of the unimportant tasks is forcing us to do them first. There seems to be no limit to the excuses that people come up with for putting off something that should be done now.

I've never seen figures on how much money is lost in this country through procrastination, but it must be in the billions. Check the line-ups at the post office on the last day for tax returns, or the final day for anything for that matter. According to one author, an estimated 10 million people in the U.S. buy their Valentine's Day gift or card on February 14th.

A procrastinator's view of time is distorted. They feel there's plenty of time in the future to work on their goals. Even a two week deadline seems like plenty of time. Why there's days left yet! They don't seem to come to grips with the fact that time is finite. There's only so much time in a day, month, year or lifetime. Some people actually put off living until it's too late. Of all the consequences of procrastination, the worst of all has to be cheating ourselves of the opportunity to experience life fully.

Consequences can be either external, internal or both. External consequences include things such as a fine for overdue library books, interest charges on loans, reprimands by the boss or family member, or even the loss of a job. Internal consequences include frustration, anger at yourself, feeling pressured or guilty, becoming self-critical, or never knowing the joy of experiencing something you long for.

You can usually spot a chronic procrastinator at work. They have cluttered desks, an overflowing in-basket, stacks of unopened magazines, papers to be filed and a "To Do" list that gets longer every day. You have to continually follow up to get anything from them. They frequently cancel appointments, reschedule meetings, and cancel out of seminars at the last minute. They're usually flustered, disorganized and under constant pressure. And generally have a poor self-image.

Kick the procrastination habit

Most of us tend to procrastinate if the job is a big one. We kid ourselves into thinking we'll have a larger block of time available at a later date. But we never do, unless we actually schedule that block of time, as discussed in Chapter 4.

Many tasks don't have to be put off at all. If they don't require a lot of set-up or make-ready time, they can be completed gradually, a little at a time. The trick is to start the task regardless of whether we have 5 minutes or 5 hours. At least we can bring the task 5 minutes closer to completion. Time management expert Alan Lakein refers to this as the "Swiss cheese" method - making small holes in an overwhelming task until it looks like a Swiss cheese and is finally eliminated altogether. There's no such thing as an insurmountable task - only long links of small tasks that collectively seem insurmountable.

We never wallpaper a whole room. We paper one strip at a time, one wall at a time, until the whole room is papered. Similarly, we don't write a book. That's an overwhelming task. We simply write series of paragraphs which link together to form a chapter, which in turn link with other chapters to form a book. We must approach many large tasks this way or we will never get the courage to tackle them at all. We'll procrastinate.

For proof that the above approach really works, take a look at the many activities you *don't want* to end. Our lives, for instance, are used up only too quickly, one year at a time, one day at a time, one hour at a time. Yet how insignificant that one hour seems relative to a life-time.

Try it. If you want to move three hundred files from your office to your home, simply throw 3 or 4 into your briefcase each night. Within a few months you will have moved them all. If you have to write something involving a long, involved procedure, simply spend 10 minutes each day writing one step of that procedure. If you have to clean out a closet at home, tackle only one hanger or one carton each night.

Don't let overwhelming tasks force you to procrastinate. This was brought home to me when I was a high school graduate working in a supermarket. My older brother urged me to continue my education by getting a university degree in the evenings. When I protested that I didn't have the time or the money for such an undertaking, he suggested I take only one course per year.

"But that's impossible!" I exclaimed. "At that rate it would take me 15 years. I'd be 33 years old before I got my degree!" He was unimpressed. "Well, you'll be 33 years old anyway, won't you?" he asked. How right he was. I didn't take his advice and 15 years later found myself 33 years old, but *without* a degree. Time passes regardless, so why not go after your goals while it does.

We tend to postpone jobs that are unpleasant. If we

have to deny a request, cancel an order, or dismiss an employee, we drag our feet. And why not? It's distasteful. So we worry about it. We get upset. We feel the stress. Oh, how we loathe the time when we cannot postpone it any longer and finally have to act. But act we must, and when we finally do - what a relief! A load has been lifted from us.

Why suffer by dragging out the inevitable? Get the "do it now" habit. Don't tell yourself, "It's unpleasant, so I'll delay action." Say instead, "It's unpleasant, so I'll *do it now* and get it over with." Your effectiveness will increase because an unpleasant task isn't hanging over your head. You won't be under stress. And your prompt action may prevent further complications or embarrassment, squelch rumors, and improve relationships. Replace the procrastination habit with the "do it now" habit.

Although reluctance to start unpleasant or time consuming tasks is the major cause of procrastination, some managers are simply disorganized. They lack clear-cut goals, don't plan or schedule adequately, have misplaced priorities and manage themselves poorly with respect to time. The procrastination parasite thrives on these individuals. They are so busy hopping from one job to another and dealing with constant interruptions that they postpone everything that isn't yet a crisis.

If you were a victim of disorganization, the earlier chapters should have helped you. Have your goals in writing. Plan your months, days, and hours. Reject activities that won't lead you closer to your goals and schedule the others in order of priority. Make appointments with yourself to start each project at a particular time, and keep those appointments. Schedule those long or distasteful activities early in the day. Then get a head start by starting early. A fast and productive start sets the stage for a productive day. Practice self-discipline. Make up your mind *now* that you are going to adopt a "do it now" attitude.

Overcome absentmindedness

Ever find yourself staring blankly into a filing cabinet drawer wondering what it is you were looking for? Or trying to recall where you put your spare pair of eyeglasses? Or searching in vain for your misplaced car keys? If so, you're no different from the rest of us. Next to forgetting names, absentmindedness is the most common complaint of managers who attended my memory-training seminars. It is a time consuming habit that must be overcome. And it *can* be overcome. But it requires a conscious effort. Even persons with excellent memories can be absentminded, for absentmindedness is nothing more than inattention. If you were not preoccupied with other thoughts and paid attention to where you put your spare pair of glasses, you would remember where they were.

We must educate ourselves to do things consciously and not to allow our thoughts to wander. The first step is to make up our minds right now that we are going to make the effort. We must convince ourselves that we *want* to recall where we left things and that we *are* going to recall where we left them. Then we can assist our ability to recall by making sure we have a vivid picture of where we put things.

This can be done in several ways. One is to have a *reason* for putting something where you do. Did you put your glasses in the top left-hand drawer of the kitchen cupboard because it's the closest one to the front door? Or in the medicine cabinet because that's where you keep your spare razor, batteries, shoelaces, etc.? If you have a logical reason for putting things where you do, you will probably be able to recall the *reason* - which in turn will remind you of the *place.*

Another way is to say it aloud. "I am putting the spare office keys in the top drawer of my desk because that's where the deposit-box key is kept." Your brain listens to and remembers the sound of your voice. To reinforce it even further, make a conscious association between the object and the place where you're putting it. For example, visualize that top drawer slamming shut on your glasses, smashing them into a thousand pieces. Get action into your picture. Exaggerate. The more ridiculous, violent, and colorful visualizations are hard *not* to recall. The very idea of making an association makes you think of what you're doing for at least a fraction of a second and that's usually all that's necessary. Remember, the eyes cannot see when the mind is absent.

Memory lapses sometimes result from concentrating too much on one thing and not enough on another. When we're thinking about that important visitor, catching a plane, or giving a speech, we tend to forget the habitual things we do such as removing our eyeglasses and setting them on top of the filing cabinet or bookcase. But with a little willpower, we can get into the habit of making split-second associations.

If you bring a report with you when you go to lunch, and then set it on the chair, you can make sure you won't forget it by associating it with the check. Visualize the check with a report written on it in glaring

169

red phosphorescent ink. Or visualize a huge report nailed across the exit blocking your way. This may all sound ridiculous. It is. And that's why it works. And in time you will find you have acquired the habit of *thinking about what you are doing.*

There's no easy way of curing absentmindedness. For it requires continuing attempts to be aware of what we are doing, of where we are putting things, of things we are supposed to do, or of calls we are supposed to make. It's so easy to park the car and rush into the mall without paying one bit of attention to where we parked the car. It's easy because our mind is on our shopping or our time problem and not on the parking spot. Once we have acquired the habit of automatically picking out some landmark - a lamppost or flagpole for instance - and noting where our car is in relationship to it, it becomes easy to remember. Once we *consciously* make an association, it's easy to recall it later.

An organized person is usually better at remembering. Right now you should be pretty well organized. Just remember, always make an effort to concentrate on what you are doing. It's difficult to do this when you're constantly multitasking. So concentrate on one task at a time.

Don't be a perfectionist

Perfectionists are easy targets for humorists. For example, one of the definitions offered: Perfectionists are people who take such great pains that they give them to others. Or did you hear about the perfectionist bride, who when she swept down the aisle, swept down the aisle? But perfectionism is no laughing matter. Perfectionism breeds procrastination, time pressures, stress and unhappiness. It can fracture relationships with others and bring dissatisfaction into our lives.

Perfectionists tend to derive their self-esteem from what they *do* rather than from who they *are*. They set unrealistic standards for themselves and others, constantly pushing themselves to achieve impossible goals. To perfectionists, everything worth doing is worth doing perfectly. *They spend an inappropriate amount of time attempting to achieve perfection, even though perfection is not necessary.* And they usually lay a guilt trip on themselves if they aren't successful in doing so. Add to this the time constraints of today's hectic business environment, with fewer people and more tasks, and you get an impossible situation, one that produces frustration, burnout and a feeling of hopelessness.

There's nothing wrong with striving for excellence. This simply involves doing your best under current conditions. But it does not entail excessive attention to detail, nor beating up on yourself in the process. We all have different degrees of gifts, talents and skills. And developing our skills is an ongoing process. But we cannot expect ourselves, nor should we be expected by others, to operate beyond our current level of ability. Our best may fall well short of perfection, and that's okay.

To guard against perfectionist tendencies, we must first accept ourselves for who we are. We may have been created in God's image; but we are not God. We must do our best while recognizing our limitations. We should also budget our time, spending more time on the priorities and less on the small stuff. If it's true that eighty percent of our results are from twenty percent of the things we do, it follows that if we were to concentrate the bulk of our time and effort on the twenty percent and do a mediocre job on the eighty percent, the results would be phenomenal. This does not mean we should do sloppy work eighty percent of the time. We should do the best we can in the time that we have allocated to that eighty percent. *But the additional improvement we would get by attempting to do it perfectly would not justify the greater expenditure of time.* This is an example of the *law of diminishing returns.* Perfectionists should ask themselves, "What would be the impact on the company or my career if this project were submitted as it is?" If the answer is "nothing," it would probably be counterproductive to spend more time refining it. Let the amount of time allocated be proportional to the value of the project. And spend time based on objectives, not feelings.

Whether perfectionism has stemmed from unrealistic expectations of parents or teachers, unrealistic demands of a boss, or whether it's a habit acquired from years of seeking approval and acceptance, it can be modified if we accept ourselves for who we are, evaluate our use of time, and strive to maintain balance in our lives.

Chapter 11

Delegate for results

Your time sphere

Now comes the crunch. The previous chapters were designed to get you and your surroundings organized. By doing so, you will have reduced the time spent on routine activities without causing any additional stress. The resulting free time *must be spent* on important tasks. It's one thing having an organized desk, files, systems, and work habits. Utilizing these tools to accomplish meaningful tasks is something else.

In Chapter 1, I emphasized the fact that we only have 24 hours in each day. No more, no less. And that in order to achieve meaningful goals and be effective as managers we must displace many of the meaningless or less important activities with priority, results-oriented activities. Now I will show you how you can work more effectively by making better use of your time. Rather than extend your workday to 10 or 12 hours, you will be able to *reduce* the time spent at work if this is your desire.

The sadness of it all is that many people *do* try to extend their working day in order to get more done. And it's futile. As *Parkinson's Law* so aptly states, *work expands to fill the time available for it*. Work is not solid. It is like a gas, hundreds of particles called *activities* which expand to fill the extra space. That's the reason time management experts urge us not to work longer hours in an attempt to cure our time problem. Not only does it interfere with our family and social life, it makes us less effective because we then look upon our evenings as an extension of our day. If we run out of time while working on a project, we simply shrug and tell ourselves we'll finish it in the evening. We do this rather than utilize that fifteen minutes before normal quitting time, rather than do a *less than perfect* job, or rather than do something about our problem of having too many activities to complete in a normal work day.

Alternatively, you could work faster, cramming more activities into less time. The problem with this *solution* is that you can only compress activities into so much space. A gas can be compressed. But the more it is compressed, the greater the pressure exerted on the walls of the container.

This is what causes stress, breakdowns or worse. People put themselves under extreme pressure by cramming more and more activities into the same time container. Until, finally, the pressure becomes so great that the container explodes.

You might say, "Well I'd rather extend my day than explode!" But extending your day only delays the inevitable. If you have a larger container of time, you can cram more activities into it. And you will. It's our nature. And when the explosion finally comes you'll probably be the only casualty since your family and friends will have been squeezed from the scene long ago. Extending the time available is not the answer. It's what you *do* during the time period that determines your effectiveness, and to a great extent, your health.

The Pareto Principle in action

The Pareto's Principle, named after an Italian economist-sociologist, Alfredo Pareto, states that *the significant items in a given group normally constitute a relatively small portion of the total items in the group.* The actual figures used are 20 percent and 80 percent. *So 20 percent of your activities accounts for 80 percent of the value of all your activities.*

The amazing thing about this *principle* is that it seems to hold true for everything. Twenty percent of the salespeople brings in 80 percent of the new business. Twenty percent of the items in inventory comprises 80 percent of the total value of the inventory. Twenty percent of your callers makes up 80 percent of your telephone time. Twenty percent of your employees causes 80 percent of your interruptions. Twenty percent of your paperwork provides 80 percent of your significant results. And so on.

The figures, 80 percent and 20 percent, may not be accurate, but the principle certainly holds true in practice. Believe it. *It will be the basis of your success in managing yourself with respect to time.*

Exhibit 12 is a sphere representing the time available for your work. If it represents a week's time, it would probably have a volume of about 35 to 40 hours. Filling this time sphere are hundreds of activities. They fill the sphere like a gas - important tasks, critical tasks, unnecessary tasks, unimportant tasks - all intermingled. No matter how few or how many activities you perform during a 35-hour time period, *they always fill the sphere.* (Parkinson's Law). If you are typical of the hundreds of executives I have talked to in time management seminars, there are many, many activities squeezed into your time sphere all of which exert a considerable amount of pressure.

If you could separate those activities into categories (see Exhibit 13) you would find that about 20 percent are critical priorities that account for about 80 percent of your results. The other 80 percent of your activities consists of important activities, or time obligations, unimportant but desirable activities, and unimportant and unnecessary activities or timewasters.

Theoretically, you could then eliminate 80 percent of your activities and still maintain 80 percent of your results (The Pareto Principle). I say *theoretically* because in all probability you could not maintain your job if you did. *You cannot sacrifice even 20 percent of your results.* You probably want *greater* results.

But you can: (1) eliminate the 5 or 10 percent of the activities which are unnecessary, and (2) delegate the desirable activities and some of the important activities. This would free up anywhere from 20 percent to 50 percent of your time. You could then utilize this "spare time" by taking on more *critical* activities such as planning and innovating. You must first determine the amount of time you want to spend on your job. Then you must eliminate or delegate the activities of lesser importance and fill the void with more important activities - activities that have bigger payoffs, accomplish significant results, and move you closer to your personal and professional goals.

Take a look at what you do, and why

How do you separate the activities into the categories illustrated in Exhibit 13? How can you tell how important the activity really is? How do you decide which activities should be eliminated, delegated or retained?

Start by ruling off some sheets of paper similar to the one shown in Exhibit 14. Then have a brainstorming session with yourself and list all the activities which you perform in the course of a month. Put everything down: making the coffee when you arrive early; sorting

Exhibit 12

Your Weekly Time Sphere

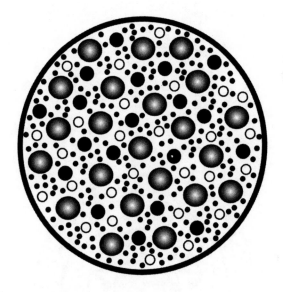

● **Priorities**

● **Time Obligations**

○ **Desirable Activities**

• **Timewasters**

Exhibit 13

Your Weekly Time Sphere With Activities Separated

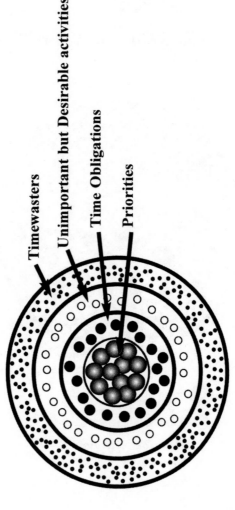

Timewasters

Unimportant but Desirable activities

Time Obligations

Priorities

through invoices as a spot check on accounts receivable; touring the plant or office on a safety inspection each week; approving overtime slips; filing correspondence; making travel arrangements; chairing a monthly managers meeting; and so on. Stay at it for a half hour or more and then leave it. Go about your work. Later, sit down, read the list and add to it. Leave it again. This time carry index cards or memo paper in your pocket and, whenever you are reminded of something else you do, jot it down. Transfer it to your sheet later. Do nothing else with these sheets for at least two weeks except to add items to the first column.

At the end of two weeks you should have quite a list, everything from ordering office supplies to conducting performance appraisals. In fact, I bet you'll be amazed at how full your time sphere really is. Do all of these activities really influence the profitability of the firm? Or the achievement of your personal and company goals? Well, let's find out.

Next, review the items in column 1, and in column 2 estimate the amount of time you spend on each of these activities. Then, in column 3, write the *reason* you personally perform those tasks or activities. Be honest with yourself. After all, nobody else need ever see these worksheets. As an example, here are some of the reasons you might jot down:

"It's my job."

"No one else is qualified to do it."

"My boss assigned it to me."

"There's no one else to do it."

"The person who held this job before always did it."

"It's confidential. I *have* to do it."

"I *like* doing it. It's fun."

"It's in my job description."
"I do it better and faster than anyone else."
"It gives me a chance to show off my skill."
"I haven't got time to show someone else how to do it."
"I don't know why. I just ended up with the job."
"I let someone else do it once and it got loused up."
"It's personal. I wouldn't *want* anyone else to do it." ...And so on.

Just the process of questioning why you do something might give you an idea as to whether you can eliminate it, simplify it or delegate it. But let's look at some of those reasons you give for doing the job yourself.

"It's my job" or "It's on my job description" or "My boss assigned it to me" are not very good reasons. Your job usually consists of a lot more responsibilities than you are able to handle by yourself. If you're a manager you're responsible for achieving certain results. The *way* you achieve them is left to your own ingenuity. Delegation is the sign of an effective manager. Changing methods, simplifying procedures or conserving valuable resources such as time and money through eliminating unnecessary jobs are all signs of an effective manager. And job descriptions are formed to *assist* employees, not to hamstring them. They can be changed if necessary. They're not carved in stone. Maybe you *do* have to perform these tasks personally. But the reason "It's on my job description" is usually not valid.

"No one else is qualified to do it" may be valid - if "qualified" means an employee has to be a ceramic

Exhibit 14

Activity - Time Analysis

ACTIVITIES I PERFORM ON A REGULAR BASIS	TIME SPENT MONTHLY	REASON I DO THESE JOBS MYSELF	CAN AN EMPLOYEE DO IT? (YES/NO)	CAN AN EMPLOYEE BE TRAINED DO IT? (YES/NO)	WHO?
1					
2					
3					
4					
5					
6					
7					
8					
9					

engineer or physicist. But if it means *training* you can always schedule time for training.

"Everyone else is too busy to do it." How about yourself? Maybe other employees need to get organized, eliminate time wasters, and evaluate *their* jobs. You can probably help them to *unbusy* themselves.

"The person who held this job before always did it" is on a par with "It's always been done this way." There may have been a legitimate reason for doing it at one time but situations change. Question it.

"I like doing it" should appear frequently if you enjoy your job. But it's not a legitimate reason for carrying on an activity that can be eliminated or delegated. There are probably a lot of enjoyable, rewarding, creative, *productive* activities you could become involved in if those enjoyable but *non-productive* jobs could be eliminated. And, if you enjoy certain tasks, just think how much your employees may enjoy them!

"There's no one else to do it" can only mean you have no employees reporting to you. And I certainly don't want to encourage upward delegation. But can you delegate it to outside resources, to your suppliers? Or can you eliminate it or simplify it, or combine it with something else?

There are probably dozens of reasons why you do what you do. Question them all. Can they be eliminated? What would be the result if they were? Don't even consider delegating a task to someone else if it can be eliminated altogether. You would only be shifting your time problems to someone else. If you've listed most of your activities, and you really question their value, you will probably be able to eliminate a dozen or more without decreasing your effectiveness.

When you have eliminated everything you can, move to column 4. Can the tasks be delegated to someone else? "Sure," you may say. "But they haven't got the time to do them." *Then make the time.* Help them eliminate, simplify or delegate some of their own tasks. Help them to get organized, utilize forms, shortcuts and checklists. Help them to eliminate time wasters. Encourage them to manage *themselves* with respect to time. Even if you have to hire an additional person (which is unlikely), it will still be more economical than getting yourself bogged down with too many essential but relatively unimportant activities. Compare the additional salary to the increased sales, reduced costs, and new opportunities that you could generate if you had the time. To fully earn your *own salary,* you must delegate almost everything except the critical and very important activities.

If the answer is still no, move to column 5. Can some one be trained to do it within a reasonable length of time? It may take several weeks. Or perhaps an hour each day for several months. But is there someone currently on your staff who has the capacity to acquire the new skill? If "yes," launch a training schedule right away. Training is one of those *critical* activities which you probably haven't had time to do properly. Yet it's a big payoff activity, one that should replace some of those low-value activities you're getting rid of.

If the answer to column 5 is "no," it's probably a critical, high-value activity or one that is peculiar to the qualifications, technical skills or confidentiality of your position. Then you can only attempt to simplify it and continue to do it.

Principles of delegation

You now have plenty of jobs to delegate. But you also have time available to train and develop your people. You must set aside a block of time each week for this purpose. First, delegate those jobs that will free up the largest blocks of your time and then the routine, simple tasks that require little training time. You will be left with even more time available for delegating the others.

Delegation extends results from what you can *do* to what you can *control*. It frees time for more important tasks, allows you to plan more effectively, and helps relieve the pressure of too many jobs, too many deadlines, and too little time. Not only that, but it is one of the most effective ways of developing your employees.

Improper delegation, however, is worse than no delegation at all. It not only creates a greater demand on your own time, but messes up your employees' time as well. Be careful what you delegate, how you delegate, and to whom you delegate. Here are a few ground rules for effective delegation:

1. Don't delegate what you can eliminate.

If it's not important enough for you to do personally, it may not be important enough for your people to do either. Respect their time and their ability. Don't waste it on nonproductive or unprofitable trivia. Your success can be multiplied a thousand times if you concentrate on the high-return jobs, and encourage your subordinates to do likewise - don't spoil it by using your people as a dumping ground for "garbage" jobs.

2. Delegate the things you don't want to delegate.

We tend to hang on to the things we *like* doing even

when they interfere with more important tasks, and even though our employees could probably do them just as well. Share the interesting work with your employees. One of the most important advantages of effective delegation is the fact that it enriches your employee's jobs. Don't limit your delegation to the boring, repetitive tasks; look for the interesting ones as well.

3. Delegate, don't abdicate.
Dumping jobs onto your employees and then disappearing is not delegation; it's organizational suicide. Delegation must be planned. Consult with your employees first; select people you think are both capable of doing the job and would like to do the job. Train them. Delegate gradually, insist on feedback, and then leave them alone.

4. Delegate the objective, not the procedure.
One of the bonuses you receive from effective delegation is the fact that in many cases the job is done better in the hands of someone else. Don't resent it; encourage it. Delegate the whole task for specific *results,* de-emphasizing the actual *procedure.* Your subordinate, under less pressure, less harried, and with a fresh viewpoint, will likely improve upon the method you've been using. Review results, not the manner in which he or she arrived at them!

5. Don't always delegate to the most capable employees.
Delegation is one of the most effective methods of developing your people. Don't continually delegate to the most capable ones or they'll get stronger while the weak get weaker. Take the extra effort to spread delega-

tion across the board, and develop a strong team with no weak links.

6. Trust your employees.
Be sure to delegate the authority as well as the responsibility. Don't continually look over their shoulders, interfere with their methods, or jump on them when they make mistakes. Be prepared to trade short-term errors for long-term results. Maintain control without stifling initiative.

Delegation is an absolute must if you are going to manage effectively and maintain control of your time. It's a critical activity and one that will increase your success.

Chapter 12

Coping with stress

Control your reaction

Let's face it, we're living in a stressful world and there's little we can do to change it But even though we can usually do little to control our environment, we can do much to control our *reaction* to it. Therein lies the secret of coping with stress.

Stress is best described as the *fight or flight response*, an involuntary body response which increases our blood pressure, heart rate, breathing rate, blood flow to the muscles and metabolism, preparing us to face some conflict or flee some danger. The body is prepared for some physical activity, but the activity never comes because most of today's situations, particularly in a business environment, call for behavioral adjustments, not physical activity. Consequently our body's systems are thrown out of balance.

The fight or flight response could be elicited when you are suddenly cut off by another car during your hectic drive to the office one morning. The body's responses prepare you for "flight" but instead you sit there and stew, your hands clenching the wheel, face flushed, stomach muscles tight. One response might be to jump out of the car, yank open the antagonist's door, pull him out by the scruff of the neck and smack him a good one. Although this would invariably relieve the tension, it is only appropriate from the viewpoint of our body's system and not from the viewpoint of socially acceptable behavior. Consequently we remain under stress long after the cause of it has disappeared.

The thoughtless motorist does not put us under stress, nor does the irate customer, the careless employee, the stubborn boss or the misplaced file. It is our *reactions* to these daily incidents that cause the grief.

Instead of saying "His attitude upset me", we would be more accurate in saying "I upset myself by my reaction to his attitude."

You can seldom control what other people say, but you can control *yourself* and how you *react* to what other people say. It's not easy. The first step is to admit that you are, in fact, upsetting yourself. Talk yourself into relaxing. Say to yourself, "Hey friend, calm down. You're starting to upset yourself again." Getting upset, putting yourself under stress, will not help solve the problem. Convince yourself of that fact. Reason with yourself. In time, you will find it actually works. But it requires a commitment on your part to take control of your own life and not to let yourself be controlled by others.

Don't let hassles get you down

Richard Lazarus, writing in the July, 1981 issue of *Psychology Today*, reported that those minor, daily events such as losing a wallet or getting caught in a traffic jam can be more harmful than those infrequent, major events such as divorce, retirement or being fired.

Those minor, daily events can have a great effect on our health. The effect will vary according to the frequency and intensity of the hassles and our reactions to them. When under pressure, those petty problems can have a much greater effect than if they had occurred at less anxious times. Stress is not caused by the event itself, but by our *reaction* to it.

Among the top hassles revealed in a survey were: *misplacing or losing things* and *too many things to do*. Time management will certainly help out with these two. Organizing yourself and your environment should alleviate the first problem, and getting rid of the trivia in your life and concentrating on priorities should relieve the other hassle.

Regardless of how effectively we manage our time, there will always be some hassles in our lives. Lazarus suggests that uplifts may serve as emotional buffers against disorders brought on by hassles. Uplifts include such activities as enjoying yourself with good friends, spending time with the family, eating out, and getting enough sleep.

And don't forget the importance of your *reaction* to hassles. If you can shrug them off or even laugh at them without letting them get you all tense and upset, you've got them licked.

Check those hassles which you have experienced during the past week. It could be you are deluged with "minor" annoyances that precipitate feelings of stress. Remember, it's your reactions to these incidents that can cause the damage:

❑ You misplaced or lost something.

❑ You spent at least 15 minutes searching for things.

❑ You have been concerned about your physical appearance.

❑ You have had too many things to do.

❑ You have been concerned about your weight.

❑ You were upset about the way in which a staff member performed his/her job.

❑ You have a disagreement with someone at work.

❑ You were stuck in a traffic jam on the way to or from work.

❑ You were involved in or present during an accident.

❑ You were dissatisfied with the quality of a job you performed.

❑ You didn't have time for breakfast one morning.

❑ You have to prod others to get on with what they were trying to say.

❑ You became annoyed at having to wait for someone.

❑ You had to stand in line at the copier, cafeteria, or to see someone.

❑ You were put on "hold" while telephoning someone.

❑ You were interrupted in the middle of an important job by the boss, staff member, or associate several times in the same day.

❑ You frequently had to respond to the telephone at inconvenient times.

❑ You were anxious to get rid of an uninvited visitor

who persisted in dragging out the conversation.

❑ You had to attend a meeting when you could not afford the time.

❑ You were held up on a task with which you were anxious to proceed because of slow decision-making or response on the part of someone else.

❑ You were given a rush job to do with an unrealistic deadline.

❑ You had to juggle priorities more than twice due to more pressing jobs cropping up.

❑ You forgot something, which caused embarrassment as well as inconvenience.

❑ You said "yes" to something which you later regretted.

❑ You had to perform an unpleasant task.

If you have checked off 10 or more of these hassles, you could be susceptible to stress-related disorders, such as insomnia, ulcers or even heart attack. But remember, it's your *reaction* to these hassles that causes the damage, so don't take them too seriously. Put them in their proper perspective. For instance, what effect is being stuck in a traffic jam and being late for work going to have on your profession, your future, and your life? Also, be sure to pamper yourself with enough of those "uplifts" that Lazarus has recommended.

Managing your health

There's more to time management than the obvious things such as goals, personal organization and delegation. The mind cannot function without a body and the body takes its share of lumps as a result of the stressful conditions under which managers must operate. We can avoid some stress and alleviate some stress, but there is no way we are going to eliminate it completely. Nor do we want to; because a little stress keeps us at our fighting best. But we can never tell when a *little* becomes *too much* and one of the few defenses we have against the ravages of too much stress is a healthy body. The most valuable resource of any manager is his or her health, and yet many of us spend more effort and money in managing our time or developing our skills.

In this age of automobiles, elevators and labor-saving gadgetry, our normal work activities do not provide the exercise which our bodies - muscles, hearts and lungs - require if they are to continue to function efficiently and effectively. An aerobic exercise program such as the one advocated by Dr. Kenneth H. Cooper will develop cardiovascular fitness and allow us to more effectively withstand the stresses of modern living. The body that isn't used deteriorates. The lungs become inefficient, the heart grows weaker, the blood vessels less pliable and we become more vulnerable to illness. Our mental state is also affected by inactivity. We become lethargic, depressed and easily fatigued.

The best exercises are believed to be those that place sufficient demand on the lungs, heart and blood system to produce the training effect. Included in this category are running, swimming, cycling, walking, stationary running, handball, basketball and squash.

If you have been inactive for a long time, it is unwise to plunge headlong into a strenuous exercise program. Many fitness institutes have excellent programs which require a thorough medical checkup prior to their commencement.

One of the safest, simplest, most effective albeit most under-rated exercises is just plain walking. One *Executive Health* report claims that walking is a significant modifier of the natural aging process. It is important to the circulation of the blood, helps protect you from the complications of arteriosclerosis, aids in the treatment of diabetes, may help induce sleep, and is beneficial in counteracting stress. The distance you go is far more important than the speed at which you travel, and the report claims that if you run hard for six miles, you burn up only 20 percent more calories than you do walking the same distance.

There is more to health than exercise, of course, and we must examine the hazards of obesity, smoking, high blood pressure, excessive alcohol and various physical and mental ailments. Regular checkups followed by corrective action if necessary and dedication to a healthful lifestyle are pre-requisites of an effective manager. There is as much, if not more, written on health than on business. Perhaps, because of this, we tend to ignore most of it and devote our valuable time to researching the literature of our chosen field. But we should re-examine our priorities. Assembling the facts, determining your present condition, planning a strategy for improvement and implementing that strategy in order to achieve your pre-determined goal is an outline for the most critical, vital and effective management technique of all time — the technique of *managing your health.*

Avoiding burnout

Keep your job, and your life, in perspective. With so much emphasis on success and achievement it sometimes becomes difficult to relax and enjoy life. Don't set your sights too high. Do the best you can, but don't kill yourself. Job burnout is a result of too much stress, and most jobs are stressful enough without adding your own unrealistic goals and expectations.

Set realistic goals. And realize that you can't do everything. Work on priorities — the 20 percent of the activities which will bring you 80 percent of the results..

And always have some way of working off mental and emotional stress. Engage in a regular exercise program. Have interests other than your job. Make it a habit to talk over your problems with a close friend. Above all, remember that who you *are* is more important than what you *do*.

It's possible that you work harder and faster under the pressure of unrealistic deadlines, but it's doubtful that you work *better*. Excellence does not come from tired, harried people. Mediocrity does. You would hate to have your plane piloted by someone who had been flying steadily for 12 hours. And you probably wouldn't feel too comfortable in a taxi if the driver had been driving all night. It's a fact that tired workers cause accidents. For the same reason, most skiing mishaps take place during that "one last run.'

Don't talk yourself into believing that working steadily with your nose to the grindstone will lead to success. It will only lead to a flat nose. Work smarter, not harder. Concentrate on the goals you set for yourself. Every day do something to bring yourself closer to them. But recognize that you will have to ignore some of those unimportant activities that produce minimal results. You can't do everything and still keep your life in balance.

Vacations should be blocked off in your calendar ahead of anything else. Relaxation is necessary in order to keep your mind alert, your body healthy, and your family together. As one educator claims, "Pausing to attend a funeral is not a time waster unless it's your own."

Some people take better care of their office equipment than they do their own bodies. The human body is a lot more valuable than machinery. And with a little care it may have a longer life. But one thing it doesn't have is a warranty or money-back guarantee. There are no returns or allowances. So spend all the time and money necessary for preventive maintenance.

To prevent yourself from filling your planning calendar with only work-related activities, schedule blocks of leisure time. Those outings with the children, that movie with your spouse, that tennis game or shopping trip. Schedule them in ink, not pencil; make them definite, not tentative. Most people schedule them with the idea that they will go through with it if *something more important doesn't come up*. And the *something more important* is usually job-related, and usually involves value in terms of dollars and cents.

Recognize that leisure time has value too. Not in terms of measurable *dollars and cents*, but in terms of long-term effectiveness; in terms of family accord and happiness; in terms of physical health and mental alertness.

The power of laughter

According to an article in the Toronto Star (March 23, 1987) humor can boost your health and wealth. Reporting on a conference on the power of laughter and play, the article quoted 82-year-old anthropologist Ashley Montagu: "Adults are nothing more than deteriorated children." When people laugh hard the heart rate speeds up, the circulatory system is stimulated, and muscles go limp.

Barbara Mackoff, author of *Leaving the Office Behind* (Dell, 1984) believes humor can help us relieve stress produced by work. And Norman Cousins, in his book, *Anatomy of An Illness*, (Bantam, 1981) gives an amazing account of the therapeutic value of laughter as he relates his own successful fight against a crippling disease. He also describes other work that has been conducted on the beneficial aspects of laughter. Although the research is not plentiful, it indicates that laughter and attitude contribute to a healthy lifestyle and possibly "cure" illness. Sigmund Freud for one, believed that mirth was a highly useful way of counteracting nervous tension, and that humor could be used as effective therapy.

As Cousins points out, the effect of uncontrollable laughter is relaxation "almost to the point of an open sprawl." It is as tangible as any other form of physical exercise. Although Candid Camera, Marx Brothers films, and books on humor were part of his self-prescribed medicine, there is another necessary ingredient. It is summed up in this statement by Norman Cousins: "I learned that a highly developed purpose and the will to live are among the prime raw materials of human existence."

An article in the Toronto Star by Paul Watson was headed, *"Laughter The Key to First 100 Years"*. The article described an Oakville, Canada resident, Rita Hubbard, who was celebrating her 100th birthday. At the time, she was still adding to her more than 2,000 hours of volunteer work and reading at least three books a week. Her secret? "I'm just an ordinary old woman, but I've spent my whole life laughing. I believe in looking on the bright side of things."

Laughter enables us to cope with the myriad of hassles we encounter every day, from irate clients to personality conflicts. According to Zindel Segal, a psychologist at *Toronto Clarke Institute of Psychiatry*, these minor annoyances can be harmful because they have a way of accumulating. All these little annoyances mount up, people become continually more frustrated and irritated. If they have no way of releasing the anger, they can become chronically upset or chronically unhappy, and could take it out on other people.

The solution? Segal suggests we try to find the humor in a situation. And put it in its right perspective. Realize you can't do anything about it, and relax.

I don't know whether there are statistics that prove that cheerful people live longer, but there's enough evidence to suggest that laughter at least improves the quality of life. So let's not take life, and ourselves, too seriously. Be quick to listen, slow to anger, and ready to laugh!

Stress will always be with us

The major time problems identified by seminar participants haven't changed much over the past fifteen years, with one exception. More people are quoting stress and fatigue as a major problem. This agrees with recent articles on the topic. One such article in the October 9, 1997 issue of *The Globe & Mail* [*Scars From Stress Cut Deep In Workplace*] by Ijeoma Ross and Gayle Mac Donald] states, "Two-thirds say their job is causing them to unravel and two per cent believe they are on the verge of a nervous breakdown, according to an *Angus Reid Group Survey*, done for the *Royal Bank of Canada.*" The article quotes psychologist Warren Shepell: "The intensity has increased and people are getting more physical illnesses. They're applying for sick leave more quickly." What are the reasons for this increased level of stress over the years? I suggest the following acronym, spelling out the word "STRESSED" represents the major reasons.

Schedules. With both parties working, sharing household chores and raising kids, conflicts in scheduling increase. Family responsibilities and social obligations, combined with demands of the job, put pressures on wage earners to be in two places at the same time.

Time crunch. A 1996-97 *Carleton University* survey of 27,000 Canadians revealed that one in five professionals now work at least 60 hours per week. The choices available to all family members, from educational courses to consumer goods, put a further strain on their 24-hour day. For example, in 1978, a typical supermarket carried about 11,000 items. Today, it's more than 24,000 items. The more choices, the more time consumed in making them.

Rush jobs. The pressures of competition and the need for instant information results in unrealistic deadlines. This is further aggravated by the impatience of people and the preponderance of "Type A" personality types [those with a keen sense of time urgency.] People feel the need to compete with one another for promotions, recognition or simply job security.

Electronics. The ease of communications produces an avalanche of e-mail, voice mail, and faxes that people feel compelled to answer. Electronics also intrudes on personal time via cellular phones, PDAs, pagers and the internet. The shear speed of transmission translates into an aura of urgency. Add to that the need to master a never-ending stream of new software and high-tech gadgets, and the stress escalates.

Staff cuts. With downsizing, mergers, and austerity programs, the work has had to get done with fewer people. Since 1980 almost three million people have been layed off by Fortune 500 companies. Not only have the remaining people had to take on a greater workload and a faster pace, they have been subjected to the stress of change itself.

Small Stuff. We are told not to sweat the small stuff; but according to psychologist Richard Lazarus, the small, daily hassles are more stressful than the major life crises. Traffic tie-ups, line-ups, misplaced items and interruptions all serve to frustrate and anger people. And people living in a high state of anxiety are 4 1/2 times more likely to die of a heart attack or stroke.

Emotions. External stress is bad enough without people sabotaging *themselves;* but they do just that when they fail to control the emotions of anger, hostility and worry. Hostility is the high-risk factor in "Type A" personality styles, and worry and anger both precipitate the "fight or flight" response, where the heart beats faster, blood pressure rises and muscles tense.

Disorganization. This is one of the major causes of stress and is responsible for many of the harmful "hassles" such as lost files, misplaced documents, forgotten appointments, rush jobs, missed deadlines and frequent interruptions. It also includes procrastination, perfectionism, inability to say no, the tyranny of the urgent and other stress agents.

What can people do to cope with environmental stress? And what can they do to prevent themselves from creating stress in their own lives? Here again is an acronym, "HELPER," that summarizes some of the suggestions made earlier, plus a few others designed to minimize the impact of stress.

Humor. A sense of humor goes a long way in not only relieving stress, but in creating a climate where the stress is not as severe. Laughter, sometimes referred to as "internal exercise," actually produces endorphins, the body's painkillers.

Exercise. Not only does exercise relieve stress, in sufficient doses it increases physical fitness and stamina so that greater amounts of stress can be endured.

Lifestyle. Those people who develop healthy habits of eating, diet and exercise are more stress-resistant. And a positive attitude, optimistic outlook, and cheerful disposition help prevent stress from gaining a foothold.

Personal Organization. Time management training helps to reduce procrastination, perfectionism and the multitude of ineffective habits that produce stress. And it is far less stressful working in an organized environment.

Expression. Calmly talking about your stress to a friend or relative helps relieve buried emotions such as anger and hostility. Also, being assertive, saying no, and honestly expressing feelings helps prevent the build-up in the first place.

Relaxation. This is the old tried and true method of stress-reduction. Deep breathing, progressive relaxation, and Herbert Benson's "relaxation response" are all popular methods of relieving tension and stress.

Remind yourself that life is too short to allow yourself to get all uptight about things you can't control. Never take yourself too seriously. Plan for the future instead of fretting about the past. And remember that you have a choice as to how you will react to life's stresses.

Chapter 13

Don't fall into
the meeting trap

Conduct effective meetings

O h, there you are Sam." You glance at your watch for the third time in as many minutes. "For a minute we thought you weren't coming." Sam apologizes in the form of a play by play description of the traffic along a five-mile stretch of Interstate 75. After listening for a respectable, but unnecessary, length of time you again take charge as chairperson. "Well, John's the only one not here yet. And we *are* twenty minutes late already. What say we start the meeting and we can fill in John when he arrives? According to Sam here, he may be stuck in traffic for quite a while." Sam nods enthusiastically and relates two and a half more minutes of traffic tales which had slipped his mind when he first arrived.

The meeting gets underway and by the time John arrives you have heard seven warm-up jokes, witnessed three treks to the coffee pot, and a good round of discussion on the first agenda item. After hearing the latest traffic report and an enlightening lecture on carburetor icing you invite John to grab a coffee while you quickly "bring him up to date." Two more jokes and a flippant remark from Phyllis Watson, the director of human resources, slip out before you get the meeting under control again. The flippant remark went something like this: "I just figured out that based on an estimated average hourly salary of $48 per hour, with 14 of us, this meeting has already cost us $720, and we've hardly got started." The remark inspired a lot of laughter.

But it was no laughing matter. The business meeting is one of the most maligned management activities in existence. It has been accused of being a time wasting, work disrupting, fruitless exercise in idleness. And improperly handled it can become just that.

Plan your meetings carefully

Meetings *can* be effective management tools. Conducted properly they can be used to gain cooperation and promote team spirit, share information, solve problems and eliminate the time consuming repetition of individual contacts. They can be used to generate ideas, squelch rumors, assign responsibilities, gain consensus and initiate action. They can strengthen close working relationships, improve morale, motivate employees and improve communications.

But before calling a meeting, make sure that one is really necessary. If a telephone call, e-mail or conference call will accomplish the same purpose, use it. Meetings are costly. (See Exhibit 15). Assuming you spend only four hours each week in meetings, over a 10-year period you will have spent the equivalent of a full year sitting in meetings. Multiply that by your annual salary and do likewise for all the other participants, and you have a sizable cost. And that doesn't take into consideration the opportunities lost by not working on profit-generating tasks during that one year equivalent. According to Doyle and Strauss in their book, *How To Make Meetings Work,* there are over 11 million meetings held every day in the United States alone. Don't add to that costly total unless absolutely necessary.

Schedule your meetings late in the day if you want it to be a short one. Business has a tendency to move quickly as it approaches five o'clock. But if you need all day and it's worth the time and expense, schedule the whole day. Successful meetings, like anything else, must be planned. And planning involves advance preparation, timing, attendance, agenda - and most important, a statement of objectives to be accomplished.

Respect the time of others by inviting only those who can contribute to or gain from the meeting. Be prepared to excuse people early when they can no longer gain from or contribute to the remaining topics.

Set objectives in such a way that you can measure the results at a later date. Do you want people to understand certain procedures, increase sales, reduce costs, or solve a problem? Include the objectives both on the agenda and on a flip chart or blackboard in the meeting room.

Develop a detailed outline or agenda and send it out to all participants well in advance. Detail the starting time, ending time, time allocated to each topic area and the individuals responsible for reports or presentations. Use a form similar to Exhibit 16 so this vital information stands out. Make it clear that any written reports should be distributed well in advance of the meeting so the participants can review them without spending valuable meeting time. When drawing up the agenda, make sure the most important items appear first. Poll the participants in advance. Make sure you know what they want discussed and what they have to report. And tell them what you expect of *them*. They should be prepared and aware of the time allocated for their presentation or report. Above all, they should understand the *objectives* of the meeting. Don't cram too much onto the agenda. Skipping quickly over critical issues in order to finish on time is *not* a time saver.

Select the meeting place carefully. It should take place away from the normal work area and needless interruptions. The room should be well ventilated, not too warm, and with enough space to allow the participants to stretch out. The room doesn't have to be luxurious. In fact, a study conducted by R. M. Greene & Associates indicated a direct correlation between room beauty and meeting efficiency - *the more beautiful, the less efficient.* Use visual aids of some kind, such as PowerPoint, flip chart or props to increase attention.

Be in control at all times

Start the meeting on time, regardless. If you're the only one there on time, talk to yourself until the others arrive! Don't recap with every late arrival. Delaying the meeting simply encourages lateness. At the start, explain what will be covered and why. Restate the objectives. Keep to the agenda and don't allow participants to take off on tangents.

If someone starts a conversation about something trivial cut him or her off politely with a remark such as "I know that problem's in good hands with you, Jack. We won't discuss it here." You might reduce petty arguments if you seat adversaries on the same side of the table, but apart from one another. If they can't see each other they won't lock horns as often. Remember, if your meeting starts to drift in a direction that will not help to reach your objective, pull it back on course. And fast. But don't get hung up on parliamentary procedure unless you're a member of parliament. The name of the game is results.

Guard against one or two people monopolizing the discussion, encourage everyone to participate and watch for those non-verbal signals that indicate someone does not understand, objects, or wishes to speak. Listen more than you talk. One study revealed that the average

Exhibit 15

How Much Do Meetings Cost

ONE HOUR MEETING						
Average Hourly Wage of Participants	Number of Participants					
	2	4	6	8	10	12
$10	20	40	60	80	100	120
$15	30	60	90	120	150	180
$20	40	80	120	160	200	240
$25	50	100	150	200	250	300
$30	60	120	180	240	300	360
$35	70	140	210	280	350	420

TWO HOUR MEETING						
Average Hourly Wage of Participants	Number of Participants					
	2	4	6	8	10	12
$10	40	80	120	160	200	240
$15	60	120	180	240	300	360
$20	80	160	240	320	400	480
$25	100	200	300	400	500	600
$30	120	240	360	480	600	720
$35	140	280	420	560	700	840

FOUR HOUR MEETING						
Average Hourly Wage of Participants	Number of Participants					
	2	4	6	8	10	12
$10	80	160	240	320	400	480
$15	120	240	360	480	600	720
$20	160	320	480	640	800	960
$25	200	400	600	800	1000	1200
$30	240	480	720	960	1200	1440
$35	280	560	840	1120	1400	1680

leader took 60 percent of the conference time. If it's one-way communication you want, forget about a meeting and send e-mail messages instead.

The meeting is over when you have accomplished your objectives, so don't let it drag on. Summarize the actions to be taken and make sure responsibilities are clear. Issue minutes promptly, with actions clearly highlighted. Ideally, a form such as the one shown in Exhibit 17 should replace normal minutes. It highlights the decisions reached, the action required, the person responsible for follow-up and the date the action is to be completed. But if you need formal minutes, use this *Meeting Action Sheet* as a cover form. Don't force people to dig through pages and pages of minutes searching for items they are supposed to look after. Chances are, they won't. And non-action is a great and costly time waster.

Always evaluate your meetings afterwards. Ask what could be improved next time. If your magic-markers run dry or the LCD projector bulb burns out and you have no spare, it should never happen the second time. *Planning for any meeting starts with the end of the last meeting.* Inadequate planning steals precious time. If you want to check the cost of this time take a look at Exhibit 18. If you have ten people in attendance, earning an average of $35 per hour, the meeting is costing you $5.83 *per minute.* If you only lose 10 minutes looking for a spare bulb or magic-marker, this simple slip in planning has cost you $58.30.

With the same table you can calculate that a 4-hour meeting will cost you $1399.20. And that's an understatement because time spent in meetings is time taken away from other critical activities. Judge the importance

Exhibit 16

Meeting Agenda

Name of group:_____

Objective:_____

Date:_____ Meeting no.:_____

Starting time:_____ Place:_____

Ending time:_____ Called by:_____

IN ATTENDANCE

IF UNAVAILABLE, RESPOND BY:

TIME	AGENDA ITEM	PERSON RESPONSIBLE	TIME ALLOCATED

of a meeting by the results you get from it. 'Cause it's costing you!

Don't attend unnecessary meetings

You must conduct meetings effectively in order to use up less time. But I'll bet you spend more time in other people's meetings than you do in your own. How do you control *those?*

Well you can't control the meeting completely, but you *can control yourself with respect to the meetings.* Don't attend time-wasting meetings. If you have doubts about the necessity of your presence, ask. Maybe you were on the invitation list so you wouldn't feel you were being passed over. There's a lot of politics at play in organizations. Some people go to great lengths to observe protocol. After all, they wouldn't want you to get your nose out of joint. "Jack, this meeting next Thursday. Is it really imperative that I be there?" That's all it takes. You may be surprised at the reply. If the person hesitates, go on to explain the critical tasks you're working on. If it's your boss, he or she is as concerned as you about how you spend your time. Maybe a copy of the minutes and a brief phone call to the chairperson afterwards is all that is necessary to keep you on stream with the meeting's objectives. But don't attend unless you feel that particular meeting is a high priority.

If the only reason you have to be there is to present a report, ask if you can attend only *that* portion of the meeting. There should be an agenda detailing the time allotted for your report. If there isn't, ask for one. And

Exhibit 17

Meeting Action Sheet

Name of group:_____

Objectives: _____

Agenda	In Attendance

Decisions Reached

Action Required	Responsibility	Completion Date

Exhibit 18

Cost Per Minute For Meetings

No. of Participants	Average Hourly Wage of Participants						
	$15	$20	$25	$30	$35	$40	$45
2	.50	.67	.83	1.00	1.17	1.33	1.50
3	.75	1.00	1.24	1.50	1.75	2.00	2.25
4	1.00	1.33	1.66	2.00	2.33	2.66	3.00
5	1.25	1.67	2.07	2.50	2.92	3.33	3.75
6	1.50	2.00	2.48	3.00	3.50	3.99	4.50
7	1.75	2.33	2.90	3.50	4.07	4.67	5.25
8	2.00	2.66	3.32	4.00	4.67	5.32	6.00
9	2.25	3.00	3.73	4.50	5.25	6.00	6.75
10	2.50	3.34	4.14	5.00	5.83	6.66	7.50
11	2.75	3.67	4.56	5.50	6.41	7.33	8.25
12	3.00	4.00	4.96	6.00	7.00	8.00	9.00
13	3.25	4.34	5.39	6.50	7.58	8.67	9.75
14	3.50	4.66	5.83	7.00	8.14	9.34	10.50
15	3.75	5.01	6.25	7.50	8.75	10.00	11.25
16	4.00	5.33	6.67	8.00	9.34	10.64	12.00
17	4.25	5.68	7.08	8.50	9.92	11.33	12.75
18	4.50	6.00	7.50	9.00	10.50	12.00	13.50
19	4.75	6.35	7.91	9.50	11.08	12.66	14.25
20	5.00	6.68	8.33	10.00	11.66	13.32	15.00
21	5.25	6.93	8.74	10.50	12.24	14.00	15.75
22	5.50	7.35	9.17	11.00	12.82	14.66	16.50
23	5.75	7.66	9.57	11.50	13.40	15.33	17.25
24	6.00	8.00	10.00	12.00	14.00	16.00	18.00
25	6.25	8.33	10.41	12.50	14.58	16.67	18.75
26	6.50	8.67	10.83	13.00	15.16	17.34	19.50
27	6.75	9.00	11.25	13.50	15.74	18.00	20.25
28	7.00	9.33	11.67	14.00	16.28	18.68	21.00
29	7.25	9.67	12.09	14.50	16.86	19.33	21.75
30	7.50	10.00	12.50	15.00	17.50	20.00	22.50

make sure you know the objective of the meeting. If there's no objective it's probably not worth attending.

People should not be subjected to lengthy meetings if only a half hour is of importance to them and if they cannot increase the other attendees' effectiveness by being present. So don't hesitate to suggest that you leave early to fulfill other commitments.

And don't forget the alternative of sending someone else in your place. It doesn't make sense to pay $60 per hour for something you can get for $15 per hour.

Be an active participant

If you have considered the above alternatives, and decide to attend the full meeting yourself, then it's probably because you feel it's important enough to warrant your attendance - and your time. But be on guard. Meetings can have meaningful objectives and timed agendas, and still take twice as long as they should. It depends on the chairperson and the other participants. And on yourself. Before you attend a meeting, be prepared. Have all your meeting material in one folder or binder. If it's an on-going committee, you should have a binder with material separated by tabbed dividers. Break down the categories as much as possible so you can find material quickly. Minutes of previous meetings should have all important items highlighted with a yellow marker. Invariably time is wasted by people searching for past records, reports or documents. If your binder is complete and properly organized, you can save everyone some time.

If you have to submit a report, complete it early and distribute it in advance. But bring spare copies with you.

There are always people who claim they never received it. (There are even a few who admit they never looked at it or forgot to bring it.)

Arrive on time but never early. Early arrivals usually get involved in non-productive conversations. Work on your routine tasks until the meeting starts. Choose your seat carefully. Avoid sitting next to the notorious joke tellers, loud talkers, or the attendees who fan all their materials in front of them to cover all the table space. Don't sit near the coffee pot, telephone or doorway or you'll be constantly interrupted. Pick a roomy spot between two introverts so you can concentrate on the meeting's objectives and help speed it along its way.

During the meeting, help keep the chairperson on track. If someone starts discussing an entirely different issue, quickly ask the chairperson if this is to be added to the agenda. And don't be sidetracked yourself. If the jokester asks, "Have you heard the one about..." quickly reply, good naturedly, "Yes, it's hilarious. Martha, on that last point, have we concluded that..." Don't react emotionally to anything being discussed. Don't allow yourself to be baited. It's a business meeting so keep it impersonal. Anger, resentment, and petty grievances not only waste time but make you less effective at making rational decisions.

Don't pass notes to the chairperson or others. Communication stops while notes are being passed because everybody's mind is on that note. It interrupts the meeting, creates a feeling of resentment among some participants, and *wastes time.* If you have something to say, speak up. But don't feel you *have* to talk. Speak only if you have something to say that will help reach the meeting's objectives.

Be an active listener and make notes. Use the *Meeting Participant's Action Sheet* to record major points, decisions reached and follow-ups required. If you have found it necessary to attend the meeting, then it's necessary to get all you can out of it. You want value for your money. You're not at the mercy of the chairperson. You owe it to yourself and the others to keep the meeting productive. For example, if you see that it's approaching lunch hour and there's only about an hour of business left to be conducted, suggest that lunch be delayed until the meeting is finished. Don't waste time on another meeting start-up unless absolutely necessary.

When it's all over, don't wait for the minutes to arrive. You may wait a long time. And you may forget what certain statements in the minutes referred to. Instead, take action right away based on the information in your *Meeting Participant's Action Sheet*. You've got the "do it now" habit. So do it.

Making meetings more productive

Here's a meeting checklist for both the chairperson and the participants. Check off those ideas you can use to make your next meeting more productive.

Participants should:

❑ Prepare for each meeting by reviewing the agenda and support materials in advance and questioning anything that is not clear.

❑ Have any reports distributed to the other participants at least one week in advance of the meeting.

❑ Contact the chairperson *before* the meeting if something is to be added to the agenda.

❑ Arrive on time and be prompt returning from breaks.

❑ Be organized. Arrive with all relevant materials easily accessible.

❑ Take notes using a form similar to the Meeting Participant's Action Sheet.

❑ Participate actively at each meeting without feeling the necessity of speaking to each item.

❑ Refrain from side conversations, passing notes or otherwise distracting others.

❑ Respect the views of other participants and receive their suggestions with a positive attitude.

❑ Resist getting involved in discussing administrative work that is the responsibility of other people.

❑ Stick to the agenda; bring up new business at the appropriate time.

❑ Use visuals where appropriate to speed up communications.

❑ Never be openly critical of others.

❑ Give credit where credit is due; this includes other participants as well as staff who prepared reports or made suggestions.

❑ Immediately follow-up on any actions required as a result of the meeting. Don't wait for the minutes.

❑ Remember to communicate between meetings.

The chairperson should:

❑ Have agreement on how to handle interruptions such as telephone calls, etc.

❑ Contact participants in advance to confirm their attendance and clarify their roles and contributions.

❑ Prepare the agenda and see that it is distributed at least one week prior to the meeting.

❑ Schedule input from guests at the beginning of the meeting so they can leave when finished.

❑ Start the meeting on time, set a businesslike but friendly tone, keep the meeting on course, and encourage participation while maintaining control.

❑ Resist the urge to recap for every late arrival.

❑ Spend time on each agenda item in proportion to the importance of the item.

❑ Remember that a chairperson is a facilitator. Make sure everybody else gets *their* ideas on the table first.

❑ Avoid covering anything in the meeting that can be read ahead of time.

❑ Watch for those nonverbal signals that indicate someone doesn't understand, objects, or wishes to speak.

❑ Call on newer employees to express their views first so they aren't intimidated by the more senior employees.

❑ Listen more than speak.

❑ Finish on a positive note, summarizing the accomplishments.

❑ Ask for any reports to be submitted *before* the next meeting.

❑ At the end of the meeting confirm the time, date and place of the next meeting.

❑ Always evaluate the meeting immediately afterwards.

❑ Review the minutes to ensure their accuracy before being issued.

❑ Follow up with the people concerned to ensure that actions decided at the meeting are carried out on schedule.

When designing the agenda:

❑ Make the agenda items detailed enough to allow the participants to prepare for each item in advance.

❑ Build in frequent breaks.

❑ Start with items requiring immediate decisions. Leave open-ended discussions until later.

❑ Highlight any changes from standard routine, such as date, time and location.

❑ Schedule topics requiring creativity and mental alertness early in the day.

❑ Avoid putting difficult topics back to back.

❑ Place time limits on all agenda items.

❑ Include ending time as well as starting time.

❑ Schedule items in reducing order of priority in the event that everything cannot be completed.

❑ Include starting and ending times and attach paperwork that will be referred to during the meeting.

Chapter 14

Make the most of business trips

Manage your travel time

Many business people are now traveling to such an extent that effective utilization of travel time becomes a major factor in success. Here are some suggestions on how to manage your travel time more effectively.

Use a travel agent. Don't waste your time or your assistant's time by encountering busy signals or being placed on hold. Or trying to decipher the dozens of possible flight connections. A good travel agent can get you to your destination with a minimum of plane changes, stops, and airport delays. Don't forget to tell the agent what you expect. Specify non-stop, direct flights where possible, connections involving the minimum delay and avoiding the busier airports. If you purchase your own tickets, consider checking your options online. Where possible, avoid arrivals and departures that coincide with local traffic rush hours. Have your tickets well in advance. Investigate contingency flights in case you miss connections. Consider flying first class or business class. It assures you of a good seat, plenty of room for work and relaxation, minimum delay in boarding and leaving the airplane and less chance of distractions.

If you travel economy class, arrive at the airport early for good seat selection. Aisle seats are more accessible. Extra leg space is available in the front row of seats and at the emergency exits. Avoid the washroom area. It will get crowded on longer flights.

Always phone the destination hotel to reconfirm your room. Check the airline to find out if the flight is delayed. Make any arrangements for car rentals in advance. Use the ones at the airports for convenience.

When packing, conserve space. Where possible,

limit your luggage to a carry-on bag to avoid waiting at luggage turntables. But be sensible when you take luggage. If you're in no hurry at the other end, don't lug a hundred pounds of luggage in the guise of *carry-on*. Be comfortable. Airlines are also becoming more strict with carry-on luggage. Have your laptop, working papers, pens etc. handy before you board the plane. Bring your own bottle of water with you. And remember, unless it's a "red eye" special, travel time is prime working time.

If you travel frequently, keep a "personal effects" kit always packed, ready to go. It should contain all those essential items such as toothpaste, toothbrush, shampoo, hairbrush - the dozen or so items most frequently forgotten. Replenish after every trip. Over packing is a time waster. Take only half of what you think you'll need. For short trips stick to one basic color for clothes. That way you can get away with only one pair of shoes and other accessories. Have standard checklists for warm weather and cold weather destinations so you won't forget anything. Exhibit 19 is an example of a typical checklist. Make up your own as you pack for your next two or three-day trip. Make duplicate copies for future use. And don't leave the job of packing until the last minute.

If you must use a large suitcase, make sure it's tough and sturdy with a combination lock. Have an identification tag inside as well in case the one on the outside gets torn off. For security reasons, don't use your home address. Identify the bags with business card addresses. Put a splash of color or bright label on the suitcase so it can be spotted easily on the luggage turntable or conveyer belt.

Consider taking a taxi or airport limousine to the airport. You can relax, read, or prepare notes en route. And you conserve time and energy by not having to find a parking space and making the long trek with a computer bag and luggage to the proper departure area. Reserve the taxi a day in advance.

Leave copies of your itinerary with your assistant and family. Include such things as the address and phone number of the hotel. While you're at it, photocopy your credit cards just in case they get lost or stolen. It's faster than copying down all the numbers.

The minute you book your flight, record the start and arrival times, flight number and seat assignment in your planner. When you actually get the tickets or electronic printout, place a check mark or other notation there. [I put a slash of yellow with a highlighter.] You will never have to wonder whether the travel agent has the tickets or whether you do, or whether you had forgotten to order the tickets. You will not have to retrieve your itinerary every time someone asks the departure time. With notations in your planner you are constantly reminded of the trip itself.

As soon as you get your airline tickets, identify them by writing the destination and date on the jacket. Place them in a predetermined spot so you'll never forget where they are. Mine go into a small "travel drawer" where I keep my passport, foreign money, maps, customs declaration forms, hotel cards etc. I have a leather portfolio, received from one of the airlines, where I keep those things needed for every trip. [Frequent flyer cards, hotel and discount cards, passport, customs declaration forms, stamps, etc.]

Fill out a customs form before you leave the house.

Always have one for the return trip as well. Frequently they don't give them to you on the plane, and you don't want to be filling out forms in the immigration area while the lineups build.

Take advantage of idle time

Some of your most creative work could be performed in airports where you are undisturbed. Join the airline clubs so you can have a place to work and a phone and high-speed Internet access. If you're having a hectic week, get to the airport early and take advantage of this interruption-free environment.

Bring along plenty of reading material and your laptop for those unavoidable waits and delays. Work on priority material early in the flight while you're at your peak. Leave reading material and routine paperwork for times when you're feeling sluggish. Always relax just before touchdown. And don't fight the crowds when deplaning from economy class. Relax. If you have luggage to retrieve you'll be waiting later anyway.

If your budget allows it, save time and effort by taking taxis rather than renting cars. Avoid the airport buses. They're usually late, uncomfortable and not conducive to either reading or resting. If your meeting or other business can be scheduled at the airport hotel, better still.

When at your hotel, review your itinerary and utilize your time wisely. You have some excellent uninterrupted time at your disposal. Bring your laptop with you so you can access your e-mail, fax memos, download articles from the Internet and polish off your correspondence.

Exhibit 19

Travel Checklist

- ☐ Hotel reservations
- ☐ Car rental
- ☐ Airport limousine
- ☐ Confirmation numbers
- ☐ Airline tickets
- ☐ Traveler's checks/Currency
- ☐ Business appointments
- ☐ Travel insurance
- ☐ Internet access numbers
- ☐ Newspapers held
- ☐ Mail held
- ☐ Security
- ☐ Pet/House sitter

Travel documents/materials
- ☐ Passport
- ☐ Customs forms
- ☐ Road maps
- ☐ Reading material
- ☐ Promotional material
- ☐ Business cards
- ☐ Working files
- ☐ Driver's License
- ☐ Credit cards
- ☐ Personal Organizer/planner
- ☐ Bottled water

Computer Case
- ☐ Laptop
- ☐ Printer
- ☐ Scanner
- ☐ Cables
- ☐ Electrical extension
- ☐ Telephone cord extension
- ☐ Printer paper
- ☐ Transparency film
- ☐ Software/disks
- ☐ Spare ink cartridge
- ☐ Cellular telephone
- ☐ PIM/Calculator
- ☐ Pocket Recorder
- ☐ Travel Box [Exhibit 20]

Clothing
- ☐ Suit
- ☐ Dress Shirts
- ☐ Ties

- ☐ Belt
- ☐ Socks
- ☐ Shoes
- ☐ Shorts
- ☐ Handkerchiefs
- ☐ Sports Jacket
- ☐ Slacks
- ☐ Sweaters
- ☐ Raincoat/jacket
- ☐ Slippers
- ☐ Bathing suit
- ☐ Jogging clothes

Personal Effects Bag
- ☐ Toothbrush
- ☐ Toothpaste
- ☐ Shaving cream
- ☐ Razor
- ☐ After shave
- ☐ Deodorant
- ☐ Shampoo
- ☐ Hair dryer
- ☐ Brush/Comb
- ☐ Nail clippers
- ☐ Hand lotion
- ☐ Lens cleaner
- ☐ Shoe polish

Miscellaneous
- ☐ Sun glasses
- ☐ Alarm clock
- ☐ Medications
- ☐ Spare eyeglasses
- ☐ Tie clip/pin
- ☐ Collapsed nylon bag

Before Departure
- ☐ Itinerary to office/family
- ☐ Newspapers held
- ☐ Mail held/picked up
- ☐ Laundry taps off
- ☐ Lights/humidifier
- ☐ Temperature control
- ☐ Keys to neighbor

Don't rely on batteries to power your portable computer when you travel. Bring along the power cord to use in airport lounges, hotel rooms. Delayed flights or changes in travel plans may produce huge chunks of work time. Include a telephone extension cord and ethernet cable. Consider having your breakfast in your hotel room (order it the night before). Use the time you save for preparing for the day's activities. It's also more relaxing than fighting the coffee shop crowds.

If you're away for an extended period of time, have important correspondence faxed or e-mailed to you at your hotel. Don't let work accumulate while you're away. Delegate if possible. Schedule time immediately after your return to dispense with any work that has been left for your return. Avoid scheduling any meetings or appointments on that day.

By planning your business trips in advance, spending a little extra money, and taking advantage of the free time at your disposal, frequent trips no longer become a major time waster.

And if you drive

If a manager works 8 hours per day, and drives 10,000 miles in a year at 40 mph, he or she spends over 31 days traveling. If you have 10 employees, each traveling 10,000 miles, you are paying the equivalent of another employee just to cover the cost of travel time. Unfortunately, we can't simply beam ourselves to our destination in Star Trek fashion. But what we *can* do is to more effectively utilize our own travel time and encourage our employees to do likewise.

Once the route has been designed to minimize traveling time, there are still several ways of productively utilizing the time still spent behind the wheel.

Professional development:
There are excellent tapes and CDs available, everything from condensations of best-selling books to motivational and sales training CDs. This is far more productive than listening to the same news over and over again on the radio. And it can reap benefits in terms of professional development. Keep a digital recorder on the seat beside you and record great ideas when you hear them.

Dictation:
Memos, reports, sales quotes, and ideas can be dictated into a small digital recorder while driving. This will reduce the time normally spent on e-mail later. It also prevents you from forgetting those creative ideas that seem to pop up out of nowhere. But do this sparingly, and never while you are in traffic. Never access the Internet or send e-mail on your PDA while driving.

Telephone calls:
On long highway trips you can get caught up on your phone calls, reconfirm appointments leave voice mail messages and return messages. But be sensitive to driving conditions while doing so. You might want to leave reminders on your own voice mail if you think of follow-ups that have to be tended to when you return to the office. But beware of concentrating on your calls to the extent that you're distracted from your driving. Make sure your cellular is hands free.

Planning:
Driving time can be utilized for planning the day,

rehearsing a sales presentation, solving a problem or reviewing and evaluating the day's activities. To be effective, however, you must be able to discipline yourself. Your mind has a tendency to wander and engage in a little extracurricular daydreaming.

Relaxation:
You mustn't lose sight of the fact that on occasion you should do nothing except relax and listen to music. It clears the cobwebs after a particularly hectic morning. A relaxation break is productive when it revitalizes you for the tasks ahead.

Quiet hour:
During a heavy traffic tie-up or when a long drive has made you particularly weary, you should consider pulling off the road and setting up office for an hour. In fact it might be a good idea to make it a habit every day - perhaps while you're still in a client's parking lot. Your computer bag should be equipped with everything you need to schedule your next day's clients, summarize reports and statistics, and update your PDA. This quiet hour in the car assures you of interruption free time away from the hustle and bustle of the office. Unencumbered with telephone interruptions and visitors, your work can be dispensed with quickly.

Tips for the road warrior

Here are a few more hints on saving time while on the road:

♦ Plan your travel route in advance. Make sure your latest calls are closest to your home or office. You will waste less time sitting in rush hour traffic.

♦   Use a checklist to ensure that you have everything you need for the trip, including change for tolls, addresses and phone numbers of new contacts, a supply of business cards, promotion material, and a bottle of water. Think the trip through chronologically as you make the list so you won't forget anything.

♦   Be sure to take reading material with you for those inevitable waits in reception rooms.

♦   Keep a record of all your calls. List what went right, what went wrong, follow-ups required, problems to be solved. And do it immediately following the call. Don't leave it until you get back to the office. Relying on your memory can be a major timewaster.

♦   If you have to travel a considerable distance to make one call, determine what other prospects you can visit while in the area. You'll reduce the travel time per call.

A McGraw-Hill survey revealed that the average salesperson spends only 39 percent of his or her time in front of prospects, while traveling and waiting time take up 32 percent. If you're a salesperson, just think what the results would be if face to face selling time could be increased to 50 percent. This could be easily accomplished if travel and waiting time were utilized to respond to letters, dictate reports, dispense with paper-work, plan, summarize sales calls, listen to CDs, and anything else that normally fills the 29 percent of a salesperson's job still remaining.

Whether you travel by plane, train, bus or car, you will encounter delays and periods of non-productive time. Your effectiveness depends on how you use it. And you will use it to your advantage if you are prepared. Equip your computer bag with standard items you are likely to need. Make it your office away from the office.

In the large pockets stow away road maps, envelopes, stationery, scratch pad, promotional material, and reading material. In the smaller pockets you might keep a PDA, pens, business cards, checks - whatever you found you have needed in the past. Make up a small travel box containing everything you've ever found you needed while on a trip: quarters for tolls; postage stamps for that card or letter; highlighter for reading material; staples; pins; and thread. Exhibit 20 lists the items I used to carry in my travel box - a plastic container which nestled neatly in one corner of my briefcase.

The more organized you become, the less effort it takes to become even more organized. And the more time you'll have for those important things in your life.

Technology can save time

As electronic equipment becomes smaller, faster and cheaper, it becomes possible to carry an electronic office in a computer bag. Although it's not always necessary to do so, I can fit into a normal sized computer bag a laptop portable printer, cell phone, scanner, power extensions, a supply of CDs, a cellular telephone, printer paper, memory stick, Palm and ethernet cable. It is possible to write and print seminar notes on site, scan items from proceedings or magazines, access the internet, send faxes and e-mail, pick up messages and remain in contact with the office, all from my hotel room. The mobile office has arrived.

If you collect a lot of business cards as you travel, a fast way to maintain your directory is to scan the business cards directly into your laptop. CardScan by Corex not only scans cards into your PC or laptop, but the software drops the name, company, phone numbers, fax, e-mail addresses and URL in the appropriate field. If warranted, you can bring the business card scanner with you. It doesn't take up much space. The names can be organized under headings, sorted, printed, exported to other programs, or transferred to a portable Palm or other PDA. Jot a note on the face of the card, and it will retain that too as it maintains a photo of the entire business card as well. It's a lot less time-consuming and more organized than keeping drawers of business cards. I find it easy to use.

If you need data at your fingertips as you travel, but don't like to lug a laptop with you, PDAs such as Palms and BlackBerrys will hold whatever information you need while you're away, icluding your telephone directory, e-mail, PowerPoint slides and alarm clock..

I hesitate to even mention specific electronic toys; because they'll be outdated before this book hits the shelves. An item copyrighted by Northwest Airlines Inc. and appearing in the April 22, 1998 issue of *USA. Today*, reported that since 1962, computers have become one million times more productive and one thousand times less expensive. In 2005 this trend continued, although not as dramatically. The point is to keep on top of the latest developments, and when you

Exhibit 20

Travel Box Contents

Fold-up scissors
Flashlight
Paper cutter
Glue stick
Stapler
Staples
Staple remover
Spare batteries
Masking tape strips
Scotch tape
3M Post-it notes
Screwdriver [for eyeglasses]
Paper clips
Pencil leads
Nail clippers
Nail file
Post-it Flags
Towelettes
Quarters [U.S. & Canada]
Tape measure
Lip balm
Sewing kit
Spare keys
Elastic bands
Name & address labels
Postage stamps [U.S. & Canada]
Band-Aids
Aspirins

recognize a gadget that will save time, consider purchasing it. No matter what it costs, it's not as expensive as time.

A word of caution

What do Brazil, Israel, Switzerland and two States in Australia have in common? They have all banned the use of cellular phones while driving. The *St.Petersburg Times* labeled cell phones "as dangerous as alcohol when combined with an automobile."

When used responsibly, cell phones are a great time saver. Unfortunately many people go overboard. Witness the following incident reported in the February 17, 1997 issue of the *Times*: "The guy was yellin' into the telephone, comes flyin' through the intersection and runs right into the back of this car that was slowing down to turn into our lot. The guy never got off the phone! He got out of his car, still talking, and stayed on the phone another half hour while the whole police investigation was going on. Police were taking their reports; he was still talking on the phone."[Eye witness report]

Although there are conflicting reports as to the safety hazard presented by the use of cellular phones in the car, the Automobile Association is adamant: "Conducting a business deal by phone, while driving a car, may further your career, but it could also shorten your life."

A study conducted by the AAA Foundation back in 1992 showed that holding a complex conversation via cellular increases the chance that you'll be distracted by about 30 percent. It was reported that one police department on Long Island in New York was issuing tickets to drivers who used a car phone while the car was in motion.

The cellular phone companies issue a manual, containing safety precautions, along with their equipment. With the increase in cellular phones, it is imperative that these precautions be heeded. Saving time is not as important as saving a life.

Chapter 15

Don't let others steal your time

Timesaving hang-ups

Yes, Ralph.. .right. . .uh huh..." You squirm in your chair impatiently. "Right... well, I'll get back to you as soon as I get word. ... " Egad! does this man never stop talking? You move the receiver away from your ear and stare at it. You can still hear the voice clearly. Monotonous. Redundant. Incessant. You join the conversation again in an attempt to end it. "Okay, Ralph. But I have to go now. Someone is waiting for me in the lobby," you lie in desperation. The voice continues, oblivious to your agony. "Oh, oh, there goes the other phone. Ralph, I'm going to have to... yes... "He's unreal! He just won't shut up. You glance at your watch for the tenth time. The one-sided conversation has been going on for over twenty minutes! "Right... Okay, I'll..." Suddenly you get an idea; you had read it somewhere in a time management book. You fight your way back into the conversation. Your voice takes on a new vibrancy. You're obviously interested in carrying on this conversation. "Well, Ralph I can see why you're concerned..." Your hand moves to the little button on the phone. "In fact I'm grateful that you called. Why only the other..." Then suddenly, in the middle of your sentence, your finger slaps down the button cutting off the conversation. You have just hung up on *yourself.*

But Ralph won't know that. Nobody hangs up on *himself.* Ralph will think it's a bad connection. He'll be frantically dialing again right now. You dash to the reception area. "Alice," you gasp. "If anyone calls I'm on the other line." Alice is beautiful. She nods and smiles knowingly. "You mean only if it's Ralph?" she asks.

241

"Yes." You sigh. The relaxed, peaceful sigh of the reprieved. "Only if it's Ralph."

Chances are, the above scene will never occur. You don't know anyone as talkative as Ralph. Or do you? Even if you do, hanging up is hardly appropriate. But make up your mind right now that people will not waste your time. You will not allow it. You did not organize yourself, your office, files, and methods just to conserve precious time for others to steal.

When driving a car you have to drive defensively. You have to guard against other people causing an accident. It's the same with your time and life. You have to guard against other people causing a time wastage. Time is valuable. The telephone is the time waster's most common weapon. So tread cautiously.

The way you use the telephone at home should be different from the way you use it at work. Its prime purpose at work is not for *socializing*. Be polite, but be brief. Ask a person how he or she is, and you may get a twenty minute discourse on the pros and cons of cataract surgery. When Jack calls, answer cheerfully, "Hi, Jack, what can I do for you?" It's not impolite, but it gets the caller to the point of the call a lot faster. Control the conversation. In meetings, a chairperson controls the conversation and keeps it on course. Appoint yourself chairperson and direct the conversation to the objective of the call. Ask as few questions as possible. It will keep the conversation short. Like a meeting, once the objective is reached, the call is over. End it politely, but promptly. Don't be afraid to say goodbye.

When someone asks for an appointment to see you, find out what he or she wants. Chances are you'll be able to settle it right there on the phone. If you have already agreed to meet with the caller, don't waste time discussing it on the 'phone as well.

The telephone is there for *your* convenience, not the reverse. You're not expected to be available at all times. Have calls screened or diverted to voice mail during certain "quiet hours" when you want to work on priority tasks. If you have no one to screen your calls, and no voice mail, get an answering machine. You can't be effective while constantly reaching for the phone, unless fielding telephone calls *is* your job. If you want the telephone to work for you, and not against you, you're going to have to observe certain timesaving strategies:

◆ Group the call-backs. Get in the habit of accumulating your messages and returning the calls in a group. Just before noon is a good time, since conversations tend to be briefer when they threaten to interfere with lunch. About 4:30 P.M. is a good time to return the afternoon calls.

◆ Dial your own numbers. It takes just as much of your time to get the assistant to place your calls as it does to make them yourself. So why waste your assistant's time as well? If the assistant can handle the complete call, that's a different story.

◆ Record the best time of the day or week to get through to the people you 'phone on a regular basis (based on experience). Include this information in your telephone directory.

◆ Don't ask for the person you're calling if you can

talk to their voice mail instead.

♦ Don't get in the habit of holding unless you have some productive work you can do while you wait. Leave a complete message on the person's voice mail instead.

♦ Before making a call, quickly jot down the points you want to discuss so you won't forget anything.

♦ If the person you're calling is not there, try to get the information you need from someone else rather than leave a message to call back.

♦ Have your assistant screen incoming calls and handle as many as possible.

♦ When your staff takes messages, make sure they record what the call is about, the telephone number, and the best time for you to call back.

♦ Arrange your call-backs in order of importance in case you're interrupted before you finish.

♦ Always have routine jobs available (signing letters, filing, etc.) to fill waiting time when making a series of calls.

♦ If some callers are long winded, try letting them talk themselves out. Silence tends to end a conversation sooner.

♦ Ask as few questions as possible. It will keep the

conversation shorter. Be polite, but brief.

♦ If you need information to allow you to work on your priority items, make those calls early in the morning to get on that person's "to do" list for the day.

♦ Make notes on all calls. They're just as important as meetings. *Use the Telephone & Visitors Log suggested in Chapter 6.*

♦ If you keep playing telephone tag, use the person's voice mail to make an appointment for the call back.

♦ If a person can't be reached by phone, try the fax or e-mail.

A telephone does not have to be a time waster. It can be a real time saver. It can save writing time. Many memos that you receive are simply asking a question or requesting information. Resist the urge to write back. Pick up the phone and give your answer verbally. It's usually faster, less expensive, and impresses the sender.

The telephone can also save meeting time. Conference calls not only save the time of the participants but also eliminate travel costs. But *you* must be in control. Don't let others use the telephone as an offensive weapon. It can be quite offensive.

Managing voice mail

Some people seem to take seriously the advice offered by Scott Adams in his humorous book, *The Dilbert Principle* [Harper Collins, 1996]. He praises voice mail since you can ignore phone calls and let them roll over to voice mail. "This has a triple advantage," he points out. "You can [1] escape immediate work, [2] screen messages to avoid future work, and [3] create the impression that you're overworked!"

Voice mail is a great time saver, but not for the above reasons. It allows you to leave detailed messages without having to talk directly to the person. On the receiving end, it allows you to receive important information while you're away from your desk, as well as provides some "quiet time" when you must work undisturbed on an important task. But it is not a screening device. When you're available for calls it should be disengaged. You should return calls promptly when it *is* engaged. Most calls should not *have* to be returned if the caller leaves a complete message with detailed information. To avoid frustration on the part of the caller, give them the option of talking to someone else in the event of an emergency.

When recording an outgoing message on your voice mail, keep it to less than 15 seconds in length. Include your e-mail address in your recording to encourage the caller to e-mail information to you instead of requesting a call back. Print your voice mail extension number on your business cards. Whether recording a message on your own voice mail or leaving a message for someone else, be sure to speak slowly and clearly. Repeat any telephone or fax numbers or e-mail addresses. People simply can't write as fast as you can speak.

Plan your calls

Plan your call before you make it. Chances are, you'll be leaving a message on somebody's voice mail and you don't want to be stammering and stuttering and forgetting half of what you wanted to say. Jot down the things you want to say or points you want to make - brief headings - on a telephone log form or stenopad or on an electronic communications form if you dial from your computer.

Voice mail is exactly that, a form of *mail*. Don't leave the person a simple message to call you back. Leave a complete and detailed message. If you must leave a message to call back, indicate in the message when you can be reached. Also indicate what action you want the person to take.

My pet peeve is that: people talk too quickly, and speed up even more when they leave their name and telephone number. Always speak clearly, slowly, and *repeat your name and telephone number.* A good practice is to write the information as you speak. If you can't keep up with yourself, chances are the other person won't be able to either.

Remember that voice mail allows you to leave a complete message without bothering the other person or getting involved in lengthy discussions. It allows you to leave instructions after normal working hours, negating the problem of time zones. Research indicates that 50 percent of all phone calls are "one way," one person delivering information to another.

Voice mail acronym

When using voice mail you want to be time-effective without being abrupt or rude. Here is a summary of suggestions in the form of an acronym, VOICE MAIL. The first word, "VOICE" applies to those on the receiving end, while the second word, "MAIL" offers advice for the callers.

Vary the message. Don't leave the same message unchanged day after day. Let the callers know there's a human being behind the electronics.

Only record essential information. People are not interested in listening to a play by play description of your day. Limit your message to a maximum of 15 seconds.

Invite people to send an e-mail messge. Including your e-mail address in the message may reduce the number of calls and assure the caller that you can be reached. You could give your fax number as well.

Call back promptly. Allow enough time each day to both review your messages and return the calls as necessary.

End with an upbeat comment. When recording your message try to sound like a human being rather than a voice synthesizer, and end with a cheery greeting.

Make it brief. Don't tell your life history, just the reason for the call.

Always repeat your name and number. And slow down. Keep in mind that someone's desperately trying to jot down the information as you talk.

Indicate when you can be reached, if indeed it's necessary to have your call returned. Otherwise you'll find yourself playing telephone tag.

Leave a complete message. Over 50 percent of calls are simply informational. Don't ask for a call-back if you can leave the information in the person's voice mail in-box.

Discourage drop-ins

Even though you're able to control those telephone callers you will still have to guard against those individuals who interrupt you in person. They could be from outside the company or they could be your boss, peers or employees.

A closed door during your quiet hour will lend you some protection. But you can't have your door closed all day.

The first thing you should do is make certain your assistant, or receptionist realizes that you don't see drop in visitors without an appointment. At least you shouldn't, except in rare cases, or you will soon lose control of your own time. Always be "busy" to unannounced callers and they'll soon get the message. On those rare cases when you want to talk to the unexpected visitors, do it in the reception area or lobby. Don't let them into your office. If they manage to barge in, stand up immediately and terminate the conversation while standing. Don't invite them to sit down and don't offer to take their coats or give them coffee. It may sound terribly impolite, but they don't deserve, nor should they expect, much of an audience if they drop in unannounced.

When someone calls for an appointment, try to settle the matter right there on the phone. In most cases a meeting isn't necessary.

If you must meet, make sure you find out how much time the visitor expects it will take. People usually underestimate the time intentionally in order to get your agreement. If they say "only about ten minutes," tell them you'll schedule fifteen 'just in case." Then make sure you schedule another appointment right after it. Don't allow open-ended visits.

If their time is up and they're reluctant to leave, use conversation terminators such as "Fine, I'll get right on it" or "Well, it was great talking to you." Turn on the old body language. Glance at your watch, close the folder, stand up. Let the visitor know the discussion is over. If you feel it's important to continue, fine. But first call your assistant on the intercom and tell him or her that you're delaying your next appointment for five minutes Hopefully your visitor will take the hint. Don't hesitate to come right out and tell the visitor that you have another appointment. It's your time. Control it.

Your own staff can sometimes be the worst offenders. Don't let them "pop in" every ten minutes. Tell them to save up all but urgent problems before making a trip to your office. Even urgent problems will usually be communicated faster by telephone. And don't forget to insist on suggested *solutions* to those problems. Effective delegation will greatly reduce the need for interruptions by staff members. You might consider a brief stand-up meeting each morning to help them plan their day and answer their questions.

It's more difficult to control interruptions by the boss. But a good boss will respect employees' time. If you have a choice, meet the boss in his or her office. That way you can leave as soon as the objective of the visit is reached. It's a good idea to have some priority task that is important to the boss waiting for you back at your office. It's a great reason for breaking away from a non-productive conversation.

In spite of your efforts, interruptions will still occur. Accept it. It's part of a manager's job. But allow for those interruptions when you schedule your tasks.

Make crises a learning experience

Crises occur frequently. But they shouldn't *recur* frequently. Not the same crises. As soon as they happen, take action to see that they don't happen again.

Planning can't prevent a crisis from happening in the first place because you can't foresee it happening. But planning must start the moment it *does* happen. You must plan to prevent the same consequences from happening again. If an item is suddenly out of stock, or a machine breaks down, or a key employee quits, then is the time to plan so the same incident doesn't recur. Or if it can't be prevented, plan so productivity isn't affected the same way.

Crises will always occur. And handling them is part of your job as a manager. But don't let the same crises repeat themselves again and again. It's poor management. It's costly. And it's time consuming.

Know when to say no

"No." is a complete sentence. You don't have to provide a list of excuses - pardon me - "reasons" for not being able to do something. Recognize that you have the right to say no unless it is clearly your responsibility. And whether you provide a reason or not is strictly your prerogative. This is not to say you should be uncooperative or selfish. But too many people back themselves into a corner, put themselves under excessive stress and unrealistic deadlines, simply because they feel obliged to say "yes" to every request.

Have as much respect for your own time as you have for other people's time. Whenever you say yes to something you are automatically saying no to something else. Something that you will no longer have time to do. That something could impact your health, family or friends.

If you feel time pressured, it's essential that you know your responsibilities and *no* everyone else's.

Others can waste your time in a variety of ways, including bombarding you needlessly with e-mail as discussed in Chapter 9. But the ones who are in a position to waste your time most are the very people you are being paid to manage. In the next chapter I will show you how you can help your employees mange their time so that your time will be protected as well.

Chapter 16

Help employees manage their time

Time wastage by employees

The *Pareto Principle*, applied to personnel, suggests that 20 percent of the people do 80 percent of the work. This seems to be supported by findings of the *U.S. National Commission on Productivity*. It reported that only two out of every ten employees work to full capacity, and that almost half the workforce does just enough to get by without attracting attention.

The above study was quoted in a 1992 book, so it's an old study. It's hard to imagine that today's employees are only working hard enough to get by. Most people report long hours, overwhelming workload and time pressures.

The Pareto Principle could still hold true, however. Regardless of how busy everyone might be, probably 20 percent of the people are producing 80 percent of the significant results. In fact, only 20 percent of the people I meet in seminars seem to be organized and working effectively. Working smarter rather than harder is the key.

Those who work smarter focus on priorities and are not distracted by trivial activities that have little impact on organizational goals. The time they spend on projects is determined by value, not urgency. They delegate, plan, and schedule time for themselves to get the important things done. They have an organized work area, filing system and work flow, They have developed effective work habits, including self-discipline and concentration, while reducing inefficient habits such as procrastination and perfectionism. The 80 percent of the people who exhibit varying degrees of disorganization, however, work just as hard or harder, put in just as many or more hours, and suffer greater stress.

Time is an expensive commodity. If twenty employees all waste thirty minutes a day, and are all paid an average of $20 per hour, the annual cost to the company will be $48,000. A survey conducted in the United States by *Robert Half Personnel Agencies, Inc.*, New York, showed the typical employee wastes about 3 hours, 45 minutes a week. At the time, this added up to a total cost of $70 billion.

If employees *deliberately* waste time on the job, they are actually stealing from the employer. And time wasting probably costs businesses more each year than all other crimes put together. Ways employees "steal" time from their employer include clock watching, frequent trips to the washroom, personal grooming, arriving late, leaving early, extended coffee breaks, personal phone calls and e-mail, net surfing, correcting mistakes, taking unjustified sick days, extensive socializing, inattention to the job, reading magazines, novels, etc. on company time, operating a business on the side, and eating lunch at their desks and then going out for a lunch hour.

Smoking, in addition to being a health hazard, is also a time thief. According to a *Toronto Star* report back in September of 1980 an average smoker wasted about one hour per day on the mechanics of smoking. And this didn't include the time lost due to cigarette-linked illnesses. The report pointed out that Canada's 65 million smokers cost their employers about $200 million a year in absenteeism and reduced productivity. And this was before smokers had to waste time vacating the premises before they could light up. So add smoking to your list of employees' time wasters.

You can deal with deliberate time wastage the same way you deal with theft or insubordination, but not all time wastage is deliberate. Employees experience most of the time problems that plague their managers. Multiply *your* time problems by the number of employees in the organization and you've got a considerable cost in terms of poorly organized time. Some writers estimate that the typical office worker is only 60 to 70 percent efficient. It is your responsibility as a manager to encourage employees to manage their time wisely. You can do this by setting a good example, making suggestions, and by encouraging employees to participate in time management programs.

Be a role model

To set a good example, you not only have to remain organized and time conscious yourself, you have to respect your employees' time as well. Don't keep interrupting your staff throughout the day. Have a brief meeting with each of them early in the morning or late in the day and pass on all the assignments at once. Don't keep delegating if they're already overloaded, spread the tasks around. And be more interested in eliminating jobs than delegating them. Use this brief communications meeting to receive feedback, ideas, to juggle priorities, and plan the day. Leave a copy of your week's schedule with them. Tell them when you'll be away. Describe major projects you've got on the go. Tell them what important visitors are expected. Your employees are members of your team. Time management within a company requires team effort.

Don't keep your employees waiting while you finish one more thing" or make "one more call." When they're in your office at your request, respect their time. When you make assignments be sure they have deadlines agreeable to both you and the delegatees. Don't be a perfectionist. Results are what you're after. Who cares if the i's aren't dotted or there's a typographical error in a report that never leaves the company. Correct it by hand rather than send it back.

Continually make suggestions to your employees as to how they can save time and increase effectiveness. And make it obvious that you want them to make suggestions to *you* as well. Share ideas. Provide training. Make time management an ongoing program within your organization similar to those being conducted in the area of safety. Keep your employees time conscious.

Don't assume that all your employees are equally motivated or equally disciplined. Courses should be directed more to the individual than to the masses, with pre-program questionnaires and interviews. Delivery is as important as content since participants must be helped to feel motivated to introduce the suggested changes into their lives. Content should include a generous serving of "how-to's" in the area of habit-forming for those individuals who have not had the advantage of an organized upbringing.

Don't insist on sending only your least productive employees to time management seminars. They are the ones who will get the least out of them. If it's true that 80 percent of the results are obtained by only 20 percent of the people, then it follows that an incremental increase in applied skills on the part of these individuals will produce a monumental increase in total productivity. Invest your money where it will do the most good.

How your assistant can help you

You may not *have* an assistant; but if you do, you'd better have a good one. An assistant can double your effectiveness or impede it. So make sure you develop your assistant to the extent that "secretary" is a misnomer. He or she helps keep you organized, assists in decision-making, keeps low-priority material off your desk, accepts responsibility, anticipates your needs, shows initiative, creates and plans. Your assistant is part of the management team and as such should participate in management development programs.

Don't settle for a word processor, file clerk or receptionist. Develop a management assistant. Time invested here will be time well spent. In addition to the routine tasks such as filing and word processing, here is what an assistant should do for you:

◆ Intercept the mail and e-mail, take appropriate action, reply to routine memos and send a copy of the reply to you before filing.

◆ Formulate replies to the more important correspondence that you would be expected to answer personally and pass it on to you for approval and signature. Or gather necessary information to allow you to reply quickly.

◆ Review minutes of all meetings, highlight those sections requiring your attention and take action on those items not requiring your personal attention.

◆ Screen all telephone calls and visitors. Handle everything possible without disturbing you. Pass on those messages requiring your attention to you, along with files or other information you may need in order to handle them.

◆ Acknowledge and, where possible handle, all memos and e-mail during your vacation or extended absence.

◆ Arrange meetings and conferences on your behalf, including hotel arrangements, meeting notices, and follow-up.

◆ Make all travel arrangements for you, including transportation, hotel, car rental, and provide you with a detailed itinerary.

◆ Maintain a follow-up system to ensure that action is initiated well in advance in preparation for meetings, trips, and major activities.

◆ Keep watch on your time. Rescue you from visitors who overstay their time, non-productive meetings that go too long, and callers who won't get off the phone.

◆ Participate in decision-making, planning, the organization of office furniture, inventory control, development of filing systems, and purchasing of equipment and supplies.

Review all time management systems with your assistant. Work together as a team. Hold stand-up meetings each morning to keep each other up to date. Encourage professional development. Pay well. And your "time" will have a personal bodyguard.

Provide computer training

People are spending so much time with computers, it's essential that they are able to maneuver quickly within each program. Shortcuts can produce considerable savings of both time and money. Employee training can yield high returns. The market is deluged with contact management, organizer and scheduling programs, to the point where it's difficult to know which one is best. Although it's important to keep updated, instead of spending so much time trying different programs, I suggest that you and your employees spend the time learning the intricacies of the programs you *do* have. People probably only use about 20 percent of the capability of their current programs. This is true for software, such as WordPerfect, Word, Excel etc. Training is a good investment of time.

The proper computer equipment can also make a big difference. A brief article in the July, 1996 issue of *Executive Edge* newsletter [800-765-4425] related the claims of computer experts Bill Planey and Doric Earle that 13 minutes per day is wasted due to small monitors. They claim that small screens increase the time it takes to move windows around, shift palettes, etc.

An article in *The Financial Post* [June10,1997], described how Clearnet Communications Inc. takes advantage of the flexibility of notebooks to increase the effectiveness of their staff. All new employees are issued a Toshiba 430 series Satellite Pro which allows them to be productive in planes, at meetings [note-taking], making presentations or at home. Many employees combine the notebook with a MIKE phone, a combination of cellular, paging and dispatching technology launched by Clearnet in October, 1996. The cost of buying notebooks is not much different than desktop PCs, and with docking stations can perform the same functions.

I saved time when I bought a cordless mouse for my laptop and stopped using the awkward little mouse pad that came with the laptop. It was easier to manipulate, faster to scroll, and a lot less frustrating. A further saving took place when I upgraded to a laptop with a built-in DVD burner, additional memory and larger screen. We must accept the fact that we'll never catch up to technology. By the time I finish typing this manuscript, voice activated software will probably be perfected to the extent that I would be able to "write" the book in a fraction of the time. That's life. It will serve me well with the next book. At least I'm not using a self-correcting typewriter, as was the case with the first manuscript back in 1980.

The next time you are working at your computer, ask yourself what would make the job easier, faster and therefore less expensive. It could be you need more speed, memory, additional features, updated software or new equipment; or simply some training.

Encourage both efficiency and effectiveness

Most people are familiar with the distinction between efficiency and effectiveness. The most frequently used differentiation is that *efficiency is doing something in the best possible way, while effectiveness is doing the best possible thing.* But too many people emphasize the importance of effectiveness while downplaying the importance of efficiency. Both are important.

Effectiveness involves having a vision or mission, goals compatible with that vision, and a plan of action to achieve those goals or objectives. But efficiency is necessary to carry out the step-by-step action plan in the most economical, expedient way with a resultant quality consistent with the goal. A goal and plan are useless if the job never gets done. Efficiency cuts through procrastination, perfectionism and inertia, and converts a plan into action. Efficiency minimizes delays, interruptions, distractions and ensures that results are obtained.

Efficiency and effectiveness work in tandem; one is useless without the other. Without effectiveness, we lack direction, drift away from the priorities, and become busy without accomplishing the 20 percent of the tasks which represent 80 percent of the value. On the other hand, without efficiency we experience the frustration of knowing exactly where we want to go, but seeing little progress in that direction. It's a two steps forward and one step backwards process.

Effectiveness has an eye to the future while efficiency deals with the here and now. A manager who is effective, sets goals. plans, organizes, directs, controls and innovates. The one who is efficient conducts the "doing" portion of his or her job with a minimum of interruptions, idle time, procrastination, indecision, perfectionism, and wasted effort.

Efficiency looks at the process through a microscope, analyzing every detail of the jobs to eliminate, simplify, combine, or improve segments of it so the total process can be accomplished in a minimum of time at minimum cost with minimum effort. Effectiveness looks at a process through a wide-angle lens, observing how it affects the productivity of the other processes, how it contributes to the goals of the organization and how it impacts the bottom line.

Efficiency studies may lead to an improvement in a process or job. Effectiveness studies may serve to eliminate it. Although both are important, effectiveness studies should come first, since there's little point in improving something that may later be eliminated. Never underestimate the importance of efficiency; but never strive for efficiency at the expense of effectiveness.

The higher the level in the organization, the more time a manager must spend managing, and less time actually doing. Therefore, effectiveness becomes more essential at higher levels in the organization, while efficiency is critical at the staff level. But even a CEO has a certain amount of *doing* and limited time for its accomplishment. Efficiency never loses its importance.

Although time management experts urge us not to be efficient at the expense of effectiveness, this should not be construed to mean efficiency is unimportant. Lacking effectiveness is like sailing a ship without a rudder. But it is no less serious to be sailing a rudder without a ship.

Motivate through delegation

Most of us are aware of the advantages of being able to delegate to others. It not only frees up our time to work on other priorities, it also develops other people's skills and motivates them to work more effectively. The more control you give to others, the less stress they experience. But dumping jobs onto others, with little planning, training or feedback, is neither motivational nor stress-reducing. I have already discussed delegation in Chapter 11, but here are a few more suggestions from the perspective of motivating employees and helping them to be more productive.

Don't be too quick to assume people are not capable of taking on more responsibility. Individuals may lack motivation, but not ability. You cannot delegate to someone who is incapable of doing the task. But how do you know whether the person is incapable or simply not motivated? Andrew Grove, author of *High Output Management*, suggests you ask yourself this question: "If the person's life depended on it, could he or she do it? If the answer is 'yes', that person is not motivated. If the answer is 'no,' the person is not capable."

Lack of motivation is a problem; because you cannot force someone to be motivated, unless it's through coercion, bribery, threats, etc. And then it would be even *more* of a problem. Motivation is from within. But at least we can create an environment in which employees are more likely to be motivated. This is true in the way we delegate as well. Here are a few suggestions, in the form of an acronym that spells out the word "DELEGATE." They are based on information contained in my book, *Delegate: The Key To Successful Management* [Stoddart Publishing, 1989].

Don't always delegate to your most capable employees. Use delegation to develop *all* your people, forming a strong team with no weak links.

Every task you delegate should not be a simple, boring,

repetitive task. Share some of the more enjoyable tasks with your staff members.

Let your people make a few mistakes; don't expect perfection, and don't jump on them every time they slip up.

Encourage your staff to find better ways of performing a task once they have mastered it.

Give credit for jobs well done; but absorb the blame when criticized from above. Act as a buffer and provide feedback in the form of suggestions for improvement rather than criticism.

Ask for solutions, not problems. Encourage your staff to think for themselves by asking for their suggestions rather than presenting them with answers to their questions.

Trust your employees; don't over supervise. Initially be willing to accept less than you would have accomplished yourself. Be prepared to trade short-term errors for long-term results.

Endeavor to provide as much information as needed to perform the task. Communicate clearly your expectations, including deadlines and type of feedback required. Don't rush the delegation process.

The most important requirement in motivation is to know your people. What are their personal goals? What is important to them? You cannot assume your employees are motivated by money, nor can you assume they *are not* motivated by money. Each individual is unique in some respects. However, they are basically goal-oriented, whether they realize it or not. If you can help them achieve their goals, you're likely to have motivated employees.

Find out where your people stand. Talk to them, observe them and above all, *listen* to them. If their goals are compatible with the organization, great. And if their personal goals can be achieved through the job they are performing in the organization, terrific! You may have to change the nature of the job, reassign them, or even replace them. The most important factor in job motivation is the job itself. And the job is enriched through delegation.

Select people carefully. Be aware of their needs, and delegate jobs which provide the sense of achievement, challenge or recognition which meet those needs. Provide sufficient extrinsic rewards such as salary, fringe benefits, working conditions etc. so they will not be distracted. Then help them to *motivate themselves* by training them, guiding them, encouraging them, evaluating them, helping them, and commending them. *Commending* reaps greater results than *commanding*.

Chapter 17

Time management in the home

Take good work habits home with you

So far I've been discussing time management as it applies to our business-related activities. Yet about two-thirds of our time is spent away from the job. We cannot expect to manage our lives by concerning ourselves with only work-related activities.

To be in control of our lives we must manage our time at home as well. That is, we must organize ourselves in our home environments in such a way that we spend as little time as possible on those necessary, yet unrewarding activities that keep us from achieving our personal goals.

Goals will he different for different people. Your goals may include spending more time with the family, taking an evening course in automotive repair, teaching your children how to cook, building a rec room, and jogging every evening - whatever is important, meaningful, and enjoyable to *you*. It's unlikely you derive much pleasure from searching through the phone book for telephone numbers, picking up after the children, searching for misplaced items, and running up and down the stairs. You may not even enjoy mowing the lawn, washing the dishes, talking on the telephone or entertaining guests.

You are the only one who can determine how you would like to spend your time. But once you have determined it, you can *do* it. By being organized.

You can adapt many of the office systems to the home because many of the activities are similar. You constantly make and receive telephone calls. You write letters, pay bills, and file correspondence. You receive visitors. Delegate to family members. You read magazines and books. Schedule projects and tasks. Handle crises. Make decisions. Travel. Plan.

So just like the office, you should have some central place from which you operate. It could be an office in the basement, a desk in the bedroom, a table in the den, or even a corner of the kitchen table. It should be a place where you can schedule the occasional quiet hour, free from the blare of the TV and exuberant children; a place where you can reach the telephone, have space for a file box, writing materials and the usual small office supplies such as stapler, 3-hole punch, and paper clips. Oh yes, and a place for your *Personal Organizer*.

The *Personal Organizer* might be different than the one described in Chapter 5. It will help keep you and your family organized. It will be your reference book for everything from emergency numbers to metric conversion tables. It will be a training manual for baby-sitters. In short, an information center. It will be what you *want* it to be, depending upon what you put into it. One thing's certain, it will be a big time saver.

In a 3-ring binder place the two sections described in Chapter 5, a *Telephone and Visitors Log*, and a *Telephone Directory*. Encourage your family to use the log to enter all incoming calls and messages. Put a stop to forgotten calls or misplaced messages. This may be asking too much if you have several telephone locations and several disorganized people in your home. But persist. You might at least get everyone to make notes on a note pad fixed at each location. Have *everyone* enter their friends' telephone numbers in the directory. Next time your son tells you he's going to John Wilson's, you'll know how to reach him. And the next time your daughter has to reach you at Aunt Ethel's, she'll know how to contact *you*. Have a separate section for emergency numbers: police, ambulance, close relatives, fire department, doctor, and hospital. It will not only save time, it may one day save a life.

Make up another section for emergency repair numbers: service station, motor league, furnace, air conditioner, television, and appliances. This and other sections will save a lot of searching through old records or through the telephone directory. Enter the repair service number at the time you buy the appliance. You could 3-hole punch the warranty papers, invoices, etc. and file them in the binder as well. If you prefer using a PDA such as a Palm, the esctions just described would become categories in your *Address Book*.

Get plenty of dividers and mark the tabs clearly. The more sections, the faster you can locate the material. There'll be no need to keep writing out detailed instructions every time you have a new baby-sitter. You can have a section labeled *Where It's At* - spare fuses, light bulbs, key to the garage, and extra bedding. Include a separate *Baby-sitter* section if you want, complete with standard instructions and necessary information. A section on restaurants will also be useful. List phone numbers and addresses of your favorite take-out restaurants as well. How about a *Household Hints* section where you can keep useful information you've collected on removing stains, metric conversions, and cooking charts?

The possibilities are unlimited. Make up the sections that will help keep you and your family organized and save time. If you find you have to look up certain numbers or search for certain information on a regular basis, include it in your binder. Birth dates, family records, monthly expenses - anything you have to refer to frequently.

A Home Filing System

Those items you don't have to refer to frequently but must be kept for future reference should be filed. A cardboard file box with hanging folders is ideal. It can be tucked away on the closet shelf. Label the tabs on the hanging files with broad categories such as *Finance, Appliances, House, School, Recreation.* Use manila folders for more detailed breakdowns in each category: for example, *Finance* may contain folders marked *Bank Statements, Stocks* and *Bonds, Retirement Plan...* as many subcategories as necessary to allow you to retrieve a document or letter quickly.

Don't file for the sake of filing. Throw out everything unless you feel you'll have to refer to it again. If you have a category labeled *Credit Cards* which is broken down into the various cards such as *American Express, Department Stores, Visa* etc., file your record of payments if you feel it necessary to check each monthly statement with the previous one. But if you pay on the basis of each statement without question, why bother? Your canceled check is your proof of payment.

If you must file, you must also clean out your files on a regular basis. Don't allow fat files in your home. Set up a schedule and stick to it. If you pay your bills monthly, file and discard monthly as well. A tier of trays described in Chapter 2 can be used to accumulate mail. As it arrives, toss it into the appropriate tray. They can be labeled *Bills, Correspondence, Junk Mail,* etc. You may want to discard junk mail daily, answer correspondence weekly, and pay bills monthly. If you get mail which must be acted on immediately, label the top tray *Urgent*.

You might use a wall calendar to schedule those hundreds of important dates, activities, and chores that crop up during the year. Post it where the whole family can see it and use it. Make sure everything is marked on the calendar as they become known - school holidays, vacations, club meetings, sports events, dentist appointments, and social events. You can even schedule major household chores on this calendar such as wallpapering that spare bedroom or fixing that leaky faucet. You may want to color code the entries. But keep it simple.

Make up a list of all the regular monthly and annual chores and repairs, such things as car maintenance, cleaning furnace filters, lawn treatment, and fur storage. Add them to your wall calendar. It's a simple matter to copy these same activities on to next year's calendar. And the next. You will never have to forget anything again.

In addition to a family wall calendar you may also need a central message board. This can be a cork board, clipboard with note pad, or simply magnets and index cards on the fridge door. With active families, this communications center is necessary to conserve tempers as well as time.

Organize your home

In addition to organizing yourself, you must organize the home. Much time is wasted in the home by having to search for something only to find you don't have any left. Or running up and down the stairs. Or cleaning out the junk drawer. Or trying to locate a certain shirt, blouse or necklace. Or the hundreds of other useless activities caused by not having a place for everything and everything in its place.

A common complaint of most apartment dwellers *and* homeowners is that they don't have enough storage space. Give them ten times as much space and they'll still complain. For *Parkinson's Law* applies to personal and household articles as well - they expand to fill the space available. What you must do first is get rid of articles you don't need or use. Give them away. Donate them to charity. Sell them. But get rid of them. Then move the less frequently used items into semi-permanent storage. This applies to everything: clothes, dishes, toys, jewelry, cooking utensils, and garden tools. For example, clean out your clothes closets. Anything you haven't used for a year or more, get rid of. Store the items you use only occasionally in a garment bag, suitably marked as to contents, and move to the basement, attic, utility room - anywhere out of the way. Prime space should be reserved for those items you use frequently. Pack those special dishes (that are so special you hardly use them) into cartons, and store them on a top shelf in some secluded place. Do the same thing with bedding, silverware, toys, kitchen utensils, small appliances, etc. Make sure every carton is marked as to contents. Make up a master list of where everything is stored. Keep it in that family binder discussed earlier. Soon you will find you have more room than you need.

Effectively utilize the space you *do* have. Build extra shelves in closets, racks for shoes, storage boxes on rollers for beneath the beds, cupboards to the ceiling in laundry room and utility room, shelves beneath the stairs, and hooks on the bottom of cupboard shelves.

274

Store all your articles so they don't have to be stacked on top of one another, or shoved out of the way so they can't be seen. And have a place for everything.

One shelf or cupboard should he reserved for *spares*; that is, things that keep burning out such as fuses, light bulbs, batteries, faucet washers. Another shelf should contain only those items that keep being used up, such as toilet paper, hand soap, tissue paper, toothpaste, garbage bags, vacuum-cleaner bags, lunch bags, fondue fuel, and paper towels. Another shelf (in the laundry room) should hold only laundry supplies; another cupboard or shelf for emergency canned goods. And so on. Keep all these storage depots well stocked. Don't let yourself run out of anything. Buy frequently used items in bulk. Plan your purchases. You'll find you save at least two hours per week by not having to continually rush to the store for things you've run out of.

Store the items you use daily *in the area where they will be used.* Don't keep shoe polish in the basement if you shine your shoes in the laundry room. And don't keep burn ointment in the bathroom if you always burn yourself in the kitchen.

Your time does not change in value just because you're off the job. So don't squander it. Farm out jobs you don't enjoy doing. Buy labor-saving appliances and equipment. Have a cordless phone or plenty of phone jacks and a long extension cord so you don't have to run from room to room to answer calls. Keep a "to do" list of jobs. Schedule the ones you want to or have to do yourself. Let those necessary trips (cleaners, shoe store, barber, shopping, bank, library, etc.) accumulate and accomplish them all with one trip to the plaza or mall. Arrange your trips so you hit the bank, supermarket, etc.

when they're not busy. Plan ahead. Schedule. Keep organized. You'll have more time for doing what you really *enjoy* doing.

Are you sleeping too much?

We all need sleep in order to survive. Some of us need more sleep than others. But have you really experimented to find out how much sleep you need to be at your creative best? You may find you are spending more time in bed than necessary. Many people claim they are more lethargic if they sleep in. Inertia sets in and they just can't seem to get going. If you sleep in on Saturdays or Sundays, how do you feel when you get up? Do you spring out of bed ready to take on the world, or do you have to ease your way out of bed, stagger around the house for an hour in your pajamas, and finally force yourself to take a shower and get dressed before the morning has completely vanished?

If your reaction on the weekends is closer to the latter scenario, it's probably because you have had too much sleep. (Or you have overextended yourself the night before!) Consider what sleep is costing you. In general, it's costing you one third of your life. If you live to be ninety, about thirty of those years will have been spent sleeping! And it's hard to classify sleep as the most memorable years of your life. Unfortunately, sleep is a necessity of life. We cannot add thirty years to our life by eliminating sleep. But suppose we were to sleep one hour less each night. That adds up to over two full weeks per year. In twenty-five years we will have added a full year to our waking life. Imagine what you could accomplish in a full year of uninterrupted time! And it would be uninterrupted time because how many distractions are there at six or seven o'clock in the morning?

Perhaps you could only eliminate a half hour of sleep each day. That would still provide you with an additional 183 hours each year. Can you imagine what you could accomplish at the kitchen table in that amount of time? You could write a book every year, remodel the house, or dispense with all the paperwork you receive. Or you could eliminate the late nights at the office or that Saturday overtime.

In order to find out whether you are sleeping longer than necessary, try this. Set your alarm to go off ten minutes earlier tomorrow morning. Force yourself to get up the moment it goes off. No cheating! After about a week you will have made it a habit. Then set the alarm to go off another ten minutes earlier. Get up at this new time continually for another two weeks. If your energy level does not appear to have suffered, set the alarm yet another ten minutes earlier. You will now be getting up a half-hour earlier each morning. If there are adverse effects, you can switch back. But you may find that this new time does not affect you in the least.

The important thing now is to use that extra half hour for something of value to you. To waste it on TV, newspapers, or a longer shower (if you are already spending adequate time on those things) is counterproductive. Set yourself an ongoing project in the morning. It could be reading correspondence, writing an article, researching a report, or working on a household project that you have been putting off.

By extending your waking hours with no detrimental effect on your health you have actually extended your life span. Your *waking* life span, that is.

Don't be a packrat

If you're a packrat, you're wasting time. The more we have, the more time we spend searching through it to find something we need. The thinner the files, the easier it is to locate something and the less material we have in homes, the faster we spot what we're looking for. The fewer things we have hanging around, the less time we have to spend moving them, shifting them or sorting through them.

A packrat is not someone who keeps things that are useless; a packrat is someone who keeps things that are not *used*. So if you haven't used something in over a year, chances are it is safe to throw it out. This includes clothes, dishes and utensils, appliances and all that stuff you have stored in the basement, garage or closets. Sell it, give it away, donate it, but get rid of it.

It's easier to keep something than to throw it away; we never have to agonize over whether we will ever need it again. But if we are to be organized we must get rid of it out if we're in doubt at all. Few people err on the side of throwing out too much and keeping too little. And what good is it keeping something if we can't find it anyway? *When in doubt, throw it out* is a good policy to adopt for the future.

Having said this, I realize there are chronically disorganized people who have trouble getting rid of things. There are people and organizations who can help. For instance, the *National Study Group On Chronic Disorganization* consists of professional organizers with a special interest in chronic disoganization. They can be contacted through www.nsgcd.org. *Messies Anonymous* offers support groups for "messies" and have a 12-step program. They can be contacted. at www.messies.com. Individual professional organizers who specialize in chronic disorganization or *Attention Deficit Disorder* [ADD] can also be reached through the *National Association of Professional Organizers* mentioned at the end of chapter six.

Build timesaving habits

It takes only minutes to record a number or file a piece of paper, but saves hours of searching and frustration later. Many of us waste time on the same things over and over again. How many times have you searched for your car keys before leaving for work, or for a pencil when you were on the telephone, or for your favorite tie or earrings when getting dressed?

This could happen once, but it should never happen the second time. Take a minute to establish fixed spots where you will keep those frequently used items, and take a few seconds to replace them after each use. Build a habit of returning the keys to the holder on the kitchen wall each time you walk into the house and always return your earrings to the jewel box. Always hang your tie on the tie rack. Always return the pen to the holder attached to the telephone. It will be an effort at first, but soon it will become a habit like setting the alarm or brushing your teeth. And it will save time, tempers and aggravation.

Chapter 18

Make time management a way of life

Personal organization

Watch organized people and see how they operate. There's very little hesitation, indecision, or confusion. No double takes. No frantic movements. No frequent searching. Very little wasted motion. They are smooth, calm, and seemingly unflappable. They are in control.

They reach for files confident that the item they want is there. They slide open a desk drawer, and retrieve a petty cash pad without fumbling or groping. They answer the phone unhurriedly while reaching for a pen and *Telephone Log*. They appear calm, relaxed, and efficient. And very effective. You have confidence in them. They have a calming effect on you. They're the kind of people you would like to do business with. You know they'll get the job done. On time. Accurately. With a minimum of fanfare. They exude both confidence and competence.

These people are organized. They are managing themselves effectively with respect to time. They don't waste time on trivial matters. They don't experience the same crisis twice. They plan. They schedule. They place deadlines on all activities. They don't procrastinate. Once they've scheduled a job for a certain time slot, they do it.

They operate the same way in their personal lives. They don't make panic trips to the corner store every night to replace out-of-stock items. They don't watch TV programs they don't enjoy, or waste time searching for their racquet every time they want to play tennis. Their homes are neat, organized, and there is a place for everything. And everything is replaced in its appropriate spot when not in use. There are no boxes or barrels of miscellaneous items to dig into constantly in search of something. No tangles of skates, bicycles or ski equipment. No rags wrapped around leaky faucets. No piles of shoes in closets. No mail strewn on the table, counter or fridge. These people are seldom resented. Sometimes envied. Always respected.

You can be one of these people. But you can't do it by simply reading this or any other book on time management. Nor by attending seminars. Time management is a life-long concern involving more than common sense or gimmicky techniques. It requires a strong desire to enhance personal growth and satisfaction, to make life and work more meaningful and more rewarding. It involves a dedication to become more and more organized: to break bad habits, form new ones, and adopt new methods. It involves a continuing search for new ways to increase effectiveness by sharing ideas and experimenting. And above all, it requires self-control, self-discipline, and persistence.

It's difficult at first - as breaking bad habits always is. But then the rewards start to snowball. It becomes easier and easier and the increase in effectiveness becomes greater and greater. It's at this point when friends and associates will remark, "How can you get so much accomplished? You don't even look busy!" Busyness always disappears as effectiveness takes over.

Time for a time log

Although most people will tell you the place to start is with a time log, don't believe it. Where you start is with this book- at the beginning. Get rid of your backlog first. Get organized. Establish objectives. Plan. Schedule your activities. Establish timesaving methods

Exhibit 21

Time Log

	ACTIVITY									BUSINESS FUNCTION							NOTES
	e-Mail	Correspondence	Telephone	Paperwork	Meetings	Reading	Planning	Personal	Other	Marketing	Production	Maintenance	Finance	Quality control	Safety	Personnel	
8:00 -8:15																	
8:15 - 8:30																	
8:30 - 8:45																	
8:45 - 9:00																	
9:00 - 9:15																	
9:15 - 9:30																	
9:30 - 9:45																	
9:45 - 10:00																	
10:00 - 10:15																	
10:15 - 10:30																	
10:30 - 10:45																	
10:45 - 11:00																	
11:00 - 11:15																	
11:15 - 11:30																	
11:30 - 11:45																	
11:45 - 12:00																	
12:00 - 12:15																	
12:15 - 12:30																	
12:30 - 12:45																	
12:45 - 1:00																	
1:00 - 1:15																	
1:15 - 1:30																	
1:30 - 1:45																	
1:45 - 2:00																	
2:00 - 2:15																	
2:15 - 2:30																	
2:30 - 2:45																	
2:45 - 3:00																	
3:00 - 3:15																	
3:15 - 3:30																	
3:30 - 3:45																	
3:45 - 4:00																	
4:00 - 4:15																	
4:15 - 4:30																	
4:30 - 4:45																	
4:45 - 5:00																	
TOTAL																	

and habits. Train your employees. Delegate. Manage yourself effectively with respect to time. Then and only then, will you be ready for a time log. If you attempt to keep a log on your time as a first step, you'll never get to step two. Who's got time to record where they're spending their time? Most people don't have time to *do* the activities, let alone record them.

But once you're organized and you've saved big chunks of time, you have some breathing space. Now you can become more sophisticated in your time management and actually keep a log for two or three weeks. That's the beauty of sticking to an ongoing program of time management. The rewards become greater and greater and it becomes easier and easier to save even more time and become even more effective. It's like the old saying, "It takes money to make money." It takes time to make time. And now you've got it. So free up more of it. Keep a log on your activities for a few weeks and see where your time is really going. Then take action to reduce the time being spent on non-productive, low-value activities.

I recommend the time log shown in Exhibit 21, reproduced from *Getting Things Done* by Edwin C. Bliss, published by Charles Scribner & Sons. It's simple, easy to use, and accurate enough for our purpose. Under the "Activity" section, write in those activities you seem to be spending your time on throughout the day and week, items such as meetings, correspondence, and telephone.

If you are responsible for different functions, such as production, quality control, and maintenance -write those headings in under the "Business Function" section. If you're in sales, use this section to list your

Exhibit 22

Using A Time Log

Time	e-Mail	Correspondence	Telephone	Paperwork	Meetings	Reading	Planning	Personal	Other	Marketing	Production	Maintenance	Finance	Quality control	Safety	Personnel	NOTES
8:00 -8:15					x											x	re: new fire alarms
8:15 - 8:30							x			x							
8:30 - 8:45							x			x							
8:45 - 9:00	x											x	x	x	x		
9:00 - 9:15	x												x			x	
9:15 - 9:30				x									x				
9:30 - 9:45				x									x				
9:45 - 10:00					x								x				emergency meeting
10:00 - 10:15					x								x				re: faulty conveyors
10:15 - 10:30			x														follow-up calls re:
10:30 - 10:45			x														conveyors
10:45 - 11:00		x								x							Trade show
11:00 - 11:15		x								x							" "
11:15 - 11:30																	
11:30 - 11:45																	
11:45 - 12:00	x									x	x						
12:00 - 12:15	x											x	x	x	x		
12:15 - 12:30	x												x			x	
12:30 - 12:45								x									lunch
12:45 - 1:00								x									"
1:00 - 1:15								x									"
1:15 - 1:30								x									"
1:30 - 1:45				x													C.I.M
1:45 - 2:00				x													"
2:00 - 2:15				x													"
2:15 - 2:30			x														"
2:30 - 2:45			x														
2:45 - 3:00				x													
3:00 - 3:15			x														
3:15 - 3:30				x													Hamilton contract
3:30 - 3:45				x													" "
3:45 - 4:00				x													" "
4:00 - 4:15				x													" "
4:15 - 4:30	x									x	x	x	x				
4:30 - 4:45	x										x		x				
4:45 - 5:00	x												x	x			
TOTAL																	

clients. Expand it if you need more room. You can even use it to list the employees reporting to you. A time log should (1) tell you how much time, on average, you are spending on the various activities, and (2) tell you for which functions, departments, clients, employees etc. you are performing these activities. Then you are able to evaluate your time allocation. It's one thing to spend two hours per day on the telephone, but even more revealing if most of that time is being spent talking to a client or customer who accounts for less than one percent of your sales. Remember, you want to spend the majority of your time on the important, high pay-off activities.

Keep a few dozen sheets on a clipboard and leave it to one side of your desk. Every hour or so, check off the time spent on the activities you've listed - round off to the nearest 15 minutes to coincide with the time intervals on the log. It takes only seconds to check off the appropriate number of spaces. Exhibit 22 shows an example of one filled in during my days as an association manager. Yours should be different. Keep it up for at least two weeks. Then transfer the totals to a fresh form.

Examine the results. Ask yourself questions. Are you spending more time on meetings than you realized? How can you reduce this time? Can you delegate some of the activities you're still doing? Are you happy with the amount of idle time, personal time, and travel time? How can it be reduced? Are you spending time in areas that bring you minimum benefit in terms of personal and organizational objectives? Are low-paying customers monopolizing your time? Ask as many questions as the results bring to mind. Take action. Be stingy with your time. It's your life you're spending. Be sure you get something valuable in return.

There's no ending

Time management is not a finite skill or a body of knowledge that can be studied for two days, two weeks or two years, learned and then put into practice. Like time itself, it is never ending. It is a continuing process of managing yourself more and more effectively with respect to time.

Search out ideas, new methods, new techniques, and adapt them to your use. Investigate timesaving products. Wage a campaign against bad habits which rob you of precious time. Form new habits. Keep your goals in mind - *and* on paper - and refer to them constantly. Review them. Revise them. Make sure everything you do relates to them. For the purpose of managing yourself with respect to time is to achieve these goals. If you have no goals, you have no need to manage yourself with respect to time.

Review this book again. Take out any ideas that might help you. Put them into practice. Stick to it. As an added reminder, every few months refer to the list of 25 ideas listed below. These are the keys to effective time management. Try everything possible. In time you may find that most of the ideas are working for you. But don't stop there. Time management is neither an art nor a skill. It's a way of life.

You *can* control what you do and what you accomplish in the time you have left. Do it.

Twenty-five keys to effective time management

Don't rush. People who don't have the time to do something right always seem to have the time to do it over again. Mistakes If you can't get everything done, at least get the most important things done right.

If in doubt, ask. Inadequate communications is a sinkhole for time. Don't bluff, ask. Get your pride from a job well done, not from being able to guess what's required. Asking is faster than trying to piece together fractured communications. You are respected for your accomplishments, not your silence.

Write it down. Writing things down does not mean you are circumventing your memory, you are simply helping it to do its job. We all need reminders to prevent a myriad of essential tasks from dying of neglect. The pen is mightier than the sword, and it writes better.

Organize your work area. An organized desk is not the sign of a sick mind, it is the sign of an organized mind. People do better on exams when neatly dressed, excel in sales when well-prepared, and are more productive at work when their materials are arranged in an orderly way. Keep your in-basket off your desk to minimize interruptions and distractions. If possible, have your desk face the wall.

Plan your day. If you have no objectives for the day you will likely have a matching set of results. Plans are the handrails that guide you through the day's distractions and keep you on course. Plan what you will do at the start, evaluate progress during the day, and measure results at the finish.

Schedule your tasks. Listing jobs on a "to do" list shows your intention to work on them; but scheduling important tasks in your planner reveals a commitment to get them done. Make appointments with yourself at specific times to work on your priority tasks. And try to keep those appointments.

Keep files trim. The more you have, the harder it is to find anything. Don't keep documents that are available somewhere else. File temporarily, not permanently, by marking a "throw out" date on paper you think you may need in the future. When in doubt, throw it out. Purge all files on a regular basis.

Give deadlines with assignments. Never assign anything to others without indicating when it is to be completed. Note that date in the follow up section of your planner. Never use "ASAP" or "rush"; be specific. If it's a long term assignment, follow up at predetermined intervals.

Don't be a perfectionist. If it's worth doing, it's worth doing well. But "well" does not mean perfectly; it means it is sufficient to fulfill the purpose intended. Don't spend inappropriate amounts of time on tasks that don't require that degree of accuracy or completeness.

Have a daily "quiet hour". It doesn't have to be perfectly quiet, nor does it have to be an hour. But everyone needs time for themselves to think through a pressing problem, complete a difficult task, or allow their creativity to blossom. If the environment doesn't allow it, change the environment for an hour or so. It could be more aptly called a "focus hour."

Respect the time of others. If everyone treated others as they themselves would like to be treated, there wouldn't be the unnecessary personal interruptions, telephone calls, electronic messages and correspondence that most people are experiencing. Accumulate your questions, concerns and assignments and interrupt others less frequently.

Handle paper only once. When possible, that is. Don't even look at your mail until you have 30 to 60 minutes available to review it. As you pick up each piece of paper, either scrap it, delegate it, do it, file it, or schedule a time to do it later. The same thing applies to e-mail.

Use a follow up file. When reviewing your mail, don't throw things back into the in basket. Instead, mark the date you intend to work on it in your planner and place the paperwork in that corresponding date in your follow up file. If it is a priority, and will take a half-hour or more to complete, actually block off the time in your planner.

Don't procrastinate. Procrastination is putting off until later what is best done now. If it's too large a task to complete at one sitting, break it into chunks and do a little at a time. If it's distasteful, do it now and get it over with. Putting things off wastes time, causes stress and helps make life unpleasant for yourself and others.

Get rid of magazines. Don't let them accumulate. Immediately tear out the articles you want to read, keep them in a "Read" folder, and toss out the magazines. Or photocopy the articles if the magazines cannot be destroyed. If you're not gaining much from looking at the magazines, cancel your subscription.

Schedule family time. Don't use your planner exclusively for work activities. Schedule personal time and family time into your planner as well. Activities that are scheduled are usually the ones that get done. Make sure everyone in the family has his or her own planner. Have a family planning time each week.

Say "No' more often. Some people say "Yes" to others simply because they're available or don't want to offend. Make sure the request is compatible with your goals before you agree. Have as much respect for your time as you have for other peoples' time. Remember, every time you say "yes" to something, you are saying "no" to something else that could be done instead.

Record your telephone calls. Don't rely on your memory. Make notes in a telephone log booklet or steno pad while you are on the line. Indicate any action required on your part by jotting a note on the right hand side of the page. Cross it off when it's completed. You are less likely to be interrupted if you're writing, concentration will improve, and you won't forget to follow up. You will also have an accurate record of what was discussed.

Delegate more. This is the greatest time-saver of all; because it frees up time for more important tasks. If you have no one to delegate to, ask your suppliers to help. Or delegate to a computer. It can retrieve information for you, fax, dial the telephone, or send e-mail. Be on the lookout for time-saving equipment and supplies that will help free up your time. Don't delegate anything that can be eliminated.

Subscribe to condensed information. Receive your information in brief relevant chunks by subscribing to CDs, ezines or newsletters that provide information in capsule form. The *Taylor Time Club.*is an elctronic resource center where you can access hundreds of articles as well as audio recordings and other time management information. Subscribe at www.taylorintime.com. Utilize commute time, waiting time and travel time to review these materials.

Have one planner only. Use the same planner for scheduling both work and family activities. You only have one life to share, so keep only one planner or you will soon have conflicting priorities. Avoid the necessity of *double entry bookkeeping.* Take the planner with you when you go to meetings, seminars, on trips, or home.

Avoid stress. Recognize you can't do everything or be all things to all people. Be organized, effective and efficient; but don't go on a guilt trip just because you can't do the impossible. It's not the stressful environment, but your reaction to it, that does the damage. Your health should be your number one priority. Without it you're of little use to anyone.

Practice The Pareto Principle. This 80-20 rule suggests that 80 percent of your results are achieved by 20 percent of the things you do. Focus on the priorities, and if everything doesn't get done. let it be the less important tasks.

Put your goals in writing. Time is life. Don't leave it to chance. Determine where you would like to be in 10 years or 5 years and put those goals in writing. Then schedule time for yourself to work in that direction. Where you will be in 10 years or 5 years is determined by what you are doing today, tomorrow and next week.

Attend fewer meetings. Many people spend over half their working hours in meetings. Question the necessity of your attendance. If you can contribute or benefit equally well by writing a few notes or making a few quick phone calls, do so. Meetings frequently consume inappropriate amounts of time. And time is money.

Keep your life in balance

With all the little time-saving tips being published in books such as this, as well as those being disseminated in speeches, audio recordings, videos, newsletters and seminars, there's a danger of being distracted from what's really important in life. It's great to be able to shave two minutes from your travel time or take fewer trips to the supermarket or reduce photocopies by ten percent. But how important is that in the scheme of things? Will it make much difference ten years from now that your color coded files allowed you to retrieve last month's financial statements thirty seconds faster than normal? Or that a laundry basket in every closet saved your kids from having to make unnecessary trips up and down the stairs? Seems to me it's more important that you're still in business or earning a good living ten years from now. And that your kids have grown up to be successful contributors to society.

There's a difference in having lumps in your oatmeal and lumps in your breast. We should be careful not to focus so much on the little things that we neglect the big stuff. Our focus should be more on making our life more meaningful than on making our minutes more productive. There's no sense in saving time if we have nothing of meaning to spend it on.

I sometimes think we spend too much time saving time and not enough time living it. Some of my most memorable times were when I wasted it. Like the time I spent most of the day fishing with my brother in a lake where there were no fish. Or that afternoon sunbathing on the beach with my wife when it was so cold we had to stay huddled together under a blanket. Or those mornings watching my son skate in circles during an endless chain of hockey tryouts.

Keep your life in perspective. Life is not measured in minutes and seconds, but in activities and events. Now that I'm in my seventies, I don't think of my past as a series of minutes well-utilized, but as a series of activities well-spent. My memories are not of time but of times. I'm more concerned with being than doing.

This is not to say that time management is not important; but the emphasis should be on managing our lives, not our minutes. This involves having a personal mission, setting life goals, and freeing up time for the meaningful areas of our lives such as God, family and friends.

Sure, all those little time savers will help free up time for the meaningful activities; but not if we become so obsessed with saving time that we lose sight of the reason for saving it. Don't put yourself on a guilt trip just because you can't account for every minute. And don't feel inferior simply because you haven't bought into the latest labor-saving device. Although technology was supposed to make life easier for us and increase leisure time, it has yet to deliver. People are so inundated with voice and e-mail messages, telephone calls and faxes during the day, they are using evenings and weekends to get caught up on their important work. A 1997 Steelcase survey revealed that 73 percent of office workers do some weekend work and 60 percent sacrifice part of their weekend once a month. According to an article in the April 24, 1998 issue of *USA. Today,* "instead of easing the workload, technology is making it harder for employees to escape the office."

Modern technology will never really succeed in saving time, only in changing the way we spend it. Those of you who were born before the advent of the microwave will remember that it may have taken two hours to cook a roast; but we didn't sit for two hours watching it cook. Nor did we spend the two hours cruising the Internet in solitary. We usually spent the time in meaningful family relationships.

If we become so obsessed with the minutes, we may not enjoy the hours. Don't let the means become the objective. It's better to waste time than to waste life.

Bibliography

Adams, Scott. *The Dilbert Principle*. New York: HarperCollins, 1996.

Benson, Dr. Herbert. *The Relaxation Response.* New York: William Morrow and Company, 1995

Bliss, Edwin C. *Getting Things Done*. New York: Charles Scribner & Sons 1976.

Cooper, Dr. Kenneth H. *Aerobics.* New York: Bantam, 1968.

Cousins, Norman. *Anatomy of An Illness*. New York: Bantam, 1981.

Doyle, Michael and David Strauss. *How To Make Meetings Work*. New York: Wyden Books, 1976.

Gleeson, Kerry. *The Personal Efficiency Program*. New York: John Wiley & Sons, 1994.

Grove, Andrew. *High Output Management*. New York: Vintage Books, 1985.

Lakein, Alan. *How To Get Control of Your Time and Your Life*. New York: Peter H. Wyden, 1973.

Leider, Richard J. *The Power of Purpose*. New York: Ballantine Books, 1985.

MacKoff, Dr. Barbara. *Leaving the Office Behind*. New York: G.P. Putnam's Sons, 1984.

McKay, James T. *The Management of Time*. Englewood Cliffs, N.J.: Prentice-Hall, 1959.

Merrill, A. Roger. *Connections: Quadrant 11 Time Management*. Salt Lake City, Utah: Institute For Principle-Centered Leadership, 1990.

Rodgers, Buck. *The IBM Way*. New York: Harper & Row, 1986.

Taylor, Harold L. *Delegate: The Key To Successful Management*. Don Mills, Ontario: Stoddart Publishing, 1989.

_____*Say Yes To Your Dreams*. Toronto: Harold Taylor Time Consultants Inc., 1998.

Index

To view a complete range of time management books, products, training instruments and information, visit the Harold Taylor Time Consultants Inc. website at www.taylorintime.com.